SIMPLE
WHOLEFOODS

SIMPLE
WHOLEFOODS

100 effortlessly delicious plant-based recipes for every day

SOPHIE STEEVENS

Photography by Lottie Hedley

ALLEN&UNWIN
SYDNEY · MELBOURNE · AUCKLAND · LONDON

To Mum. You are such a legend,
and we are all so grateful for you

And to anyone needing the inspiration to eat more plants
— this book is for you

CONTENTS

Hello 8
The Wholefoods Diet 16
The Wholefoods Kitchen 22

Smoothies 46
Super Salads 70
Everyday Mains 128
Wholefood Snacks and Lunch Boxes 186
Dips and Dressings 232
Raw Treats 260

Thank you 294
Index 297

HELLO

Welcome to *Simple Wholefoods*!

If you want to thrive on drool-worthy food in all of its natural glory, this book is for you. Focused on modern, nutrient-dense family recipes to accommodate all dietary leanings, taste profiles and cooking abilities, *Simple Wholefoods* is designed to help you implement simple measures towards a nourishing, wholesome life.

With all that is currently going on in the world, there is no better time to take charge of our health. Focusing on what we can control is essential, including the all-important elements of vitality within our body. The definition of what it means to be healthy and eat well encompasses a diversity of unique pathways. I've experienced my fair share of challenging hurdles when it comes to good health, which is what ultimately led me to the plant and wellness space.

For those of you who don't know the back story, about eight years ago, I was diagnosed with Graves' disease – an autoimmune disease that affects the thyroid gland and causes a variety of unwanted symptoms. After initially accepting the standard treatment from my endocrinologist, I was left with a heavy decision. Surgery or radioactive therapy would be the only medical treatments available for me. Hypothetically, this would mean taking medication for the rest of my life to recreate the function of the destroyed thyroid. My physical health had hit rock bottom and I knew I needed to make some big changes. This motivated me to look deeper into the food I was eating. After avidly reading and researching, I decided to remove all toxic chemicals, gluten and highly processed foods from my diet. I then went completely plant-based with a rich emphasis on raw fruit and vegetables. Against all odds, after six months I was in remission. Nearly six years on, I am thriving thanks to this wholesome, plant-based lifestyle that I now passionately share through my social media, @rawandfree, and books.

The experience of transforming my diet has truly revolutionised my perspective on what it means to eat real food. I also learned that the road to becoming the best version of yourself isn't always straight, but with dedication and commitment, you can certainly carve the path.

Over the past few years it has been amazing to witness the growth of the plant-based industry and see it skyrocket from niche to mainstream. It is fast becoming a positive space so many want to learn more about.

With a global movement that is progressively focused on sustainable wholefoods, the plant-based diet has burst into the spotlight. Increasingly, scientists, doctors and the general public are recognising its superiority over poor dietary choices when it comes to creating resilient health and wellness, not to mention longevity.

Recent studies draw an undeniable connection between the meat and dairy industry and the deterioration of our environment, and this has undoubtedly created awareness of the importance of eating more plants. Although we are far from where we need to be, there are small but reassuring changes beginning to unfold that support the health of our planet and tackle the serious issue of animal welfare in the food industry. With these fundamental values in mind, I believe fresh, vibrantly hued fruits and vegetables should be the emphasis on every plate. Whatever your dietary stripe, there's no denying that eating fruits and veggies nestled alongside earthy, plant-based wholefoods will contribute to robust health, while consciously and compassionately enhancing our overall nutritional wellbeing.

The overwhelmingly positive response following the release of my first book, *Raw & Free*, inspired me to produce this second title. The gratitude and enthusiasm I humbly (and unexpectedly) received from eight to eighty-year-olds, omnivores and vegans alike, was exciting and truly rewarding. Not only were people enjoying my simple, plant-led recipes and feeling amazing, they were also openly embracing the book as a practical tool in their home. To each and every one of you who read *Raw & Free*, thank you. It truly means the world! I am continuously approached in person throughout New Zealand and messaged on social media by people from around the globe who wholeheartedly resonate with my health story as they, or a loved one, navigate their own challenging health journey.

All this wonderful feedback, my lovely friends, is what prompted me to put pen to paper once again, to bring you another valuable book centred on natural, plant-based ingredients, and celebrating the simplicity and deliciousness of including them habitually in your diet. In many ways, *Simple Wholefoods* is the sister of *Raw & Free*: each is unique, but the pair works synergistically to deliver a diversity of valuable tips and easy, scrumptious recipes that will give you a wide perspective of a wholefood, plant-based lifestyle. Above all, both books emphasise how simple it can be to make healthier lifestyle choices for both you and your family.

My goal is to normalise and create awareness around wholesome eating and make it more achievable and enjoyable to flourish on a plant-based diet. I'm certainly not a qualified chef, nor do I class myself as an obsessed foodie, but through personal experience, I have become passionate about the

importance of including an abundance of fruit- and vegetable-led meals in one's diet, whatever that may be, thus encouraging lifelong healthy habits.

My pursuit of plant-based nutrition and knowledge has inspired me to experiment in the kitchen using ingredients as close to their natural state as possible to create truly delicious food. With simplicity, nutrition and bold flavours in mind, the moreish recipes you'll soon discover are a selection of modern, game-changing family meals that are plant-based, gluten-free and refined sugar-free. Developed using simple wholefoods and all-natural ingredients, these satisfying, delectable meals will have a big impact without making you feel as though you've conquered a substantial summit!

Before you dive in, take some time to read through the following pages, which feature a range of useful material. In The Wholefoods Diet (page 16), I'll explain the benefits of eating this way, and in The Wholefoods Kitchen (page 22), I'll break down the items in my pantry and describe ingredients that are commonly used to create a wide variety of plant-based meals, including all of the delicious dishes in this book. You will then discover handy, plant-based swaps as well as my favourite kitchen equipment.

Whether you're at the beginning of your health journey, looking for the inspiration to stay motivated or seeking simple, mouth-watering nutritious meals to add to your repertoire, I am confident you'll find yourself flicking through this book time and time again.

Enjoy, and sending you all the biggest love from my family to yours!

Sophie x

◀ *Left to right, Jai, Ricardo, Milo, me and Eli.*

THE WHOLEFOODS DIET

Finding the 'right' nutritional pathway can feel complicated and overwhelming these days. The diversity of conflicting information available at the tap of a finger is enough to send anyone into a whirlwind of confusion. The one scientific truth that connects the dots for me, however, is nature. Fitting like a glove within our biological make-up, I believe the array of colourful, nutrient-dense wholefoods that nature consistently provides are the foods that align best with the human body.

As their name suggests, wholefoods are unprocessed (or very minimally processed) foods that are as close to their natural, whole form as possible. Wholefoods include fruits, vegetables, nuts, seeds, legumes and wholegrains. These highly nutritious foods retain the fibre and beneficial nutrients that are usually removed during heavy food processing. In other words, they host all the good stuff: vitamins, minerals, amino acids, digestive enzymes, and phytochemicals including antioxidants and flavonoids.

When we feel hungry, we generally reach for what our tastebuds desire as opposed to thinking about what our bodies really need. By consciously eating a wide variety of these superfoods, we provide our body with the crucial nourishment required to thrive and function in optimum conditions.

In contrast, the severe lack of vital nutrients and imbalances caused by an acid-fuelled, ultra-processed diet compromises our health and vitality. In my opinion, the substantial amount of food processing is a major factor why illness and disease run rampant in our modern culture. I am continuously perplexed at how these widely available 'foods' are allowed to be marketed so heavily and promoted everywhere in sight.

As a society, I feel we are so accustomed and addicted to eating this way that we have lost a big part of our natural intuition when it comes to choosing the appropriate foods for our bodies.

For centuries, we were fuelled as nature intended, and for the sustainability of our health and wellness, and that of our planet, I feel it is paramount we revert back to those natural foods and the simpler methods of preparing them. I strongly believe conscious, clean eating is the future of our health and longevity, and plant-based, wholefood living undoubtedly leads the way.

The Keys to a Wholesome Life

1. Ensure at least 80–90 per cent of your diet is made up of healthy, plant-based wholefoods, including plenty of fresh fruits, vegetables, nuts and seeds.

2. Emphasise raw, living foods as much as possible and include raw fruits and vegetables abundantly into your daily routine. The more live, energetic and alkaline-forming foods you eat, the healthier and more robust you will become. (Trust me, you will absolutely feel the difference!)

3. Eat more fruit. Use Mother Nature as your guide and enjoy all the seasonal fruits on offer. Fruits are simple carbohydrates (sugar) so they'll provide quick and pure fuel and energy. They are excellent foods to support brain and nerve function, superior cleansers of the tissue and they aid alkalisation to support true health and vitality. Fruits are a superfood and, in my opinion, nature's most powerful food source.

4. Remove highly processed and packaged items full of unhealthy additives from the home and adopt the following mantra: '*read* packaging *before* purchasing'. If a packet is full of unusual names and numbers, don't buy it. There is almost always a healthier wholefood alternative or the option of homemade.

5. Live sustainably, ethically and organically where possible. Eating an organic, plant-based, wholefood diet not only reduces the synthetic pesticides, fertilisers and toxic chemicals entering the body, but also supports positive ecosystems within our environment and contributes to a sustainable lifestyle that is better for the health of our planet and future generations.

6. Hydrate with plenty of good-quality filtered water. A common guideline as to how much water to drink is to aim for at least two litres (or eight glasses) per day. (Fruit is also hydrating.)

7. Reduce toxic chemicals. What we breathe in and put on our skin brings the inharmonious outside world in. Choose natural skincare, dental care, hair products and beauty products whenever possible.

8. Move your body regularly by getting plenty of exercise. Keeping active has been proven to have many health benefits, both physically and mentally.

9. Prioritise a good night of sleep. Getting adequate sleep is an important but often underrated requirement for a healthy, functioning body.

10. Immerse yourself in nature. Fill your lungs with fresh air and enjoy the beautiful sunshine.

THE WHOLEFOODS KITCHEN

Over the years, I've learned that a well-stocked kitchen is the surest way to succeed when embarking on a new food journey. This is why I have provided you with an insight into the simple staple ingredients I commonly use in my kitchen. These are the ingredients that make healthy, wholefood eating so easy and delicious. I go for wholefoods that are unprocessed (or minimally processed) and as close to their natural, whole form as possible; this means lots of fruits, vegetables, nuts, seeds, legumes and wholegrains (gluten-free).

Consider this section a helpful guide no matter your dietary preference. Whether you are new to a plant-based lifestyle or simply wanting to explore more wholesome ways of eating, you'll find plenty of useful tips in these pages. I have covered all the basics, from fresh fruit and produce to dried herbs and spices, gluten-free flours to pantry staples. I also explain a handful of ingredients I use in my recipes in a little more detail.

I'm not suggesting you need to venture out and purchase every single item listed in this section immediately, but by slowly accumulating these ingredients (many of which you will already have), I promise you will use them time and again to create a wide variety of healthy, wholefood recipes, including all of the plant-based deliciousness you'll discover in the following pages.

Seasonal Fruit

First and foremost, my home is always stocked with a variety of fresh, seasonal fruit. In particular, we always have a good supply of bananas. I usually have about four to five bunches on the go; we enjoy snacking on them and also use them as the creamy base in most of our smoothies. Avocados are also on heavy rotation; I buy at least 30 per week because we add avocado to almost every meal. Through my years of eating a plant-based diet high in fruit, I've found fresh fruit to be the best source of quick fuel and energy. Being a simple carbohydrate (sugar), loaded with antioxidants, fibre, vitamins and minerals, fruit is very efficiently absorbed and utilised by your body to energise, nourish, cleanse, hydrate and alkalise, which contributes immensely to a healthy functioning body. I strongly believe that fruit is the perfect fuel for the human body, and I like to fill my kitchen with a colourful variety of fresh, seasonal fruit for smoothies, snacks, lunch boxes, mono meals (a meal consisting of one single fruit), fruit platters, fresh juices, dessert and more.

Frozen Fruit

Frozen fruit is good to have on hand for making quick smoothies or smoothie bowls. To freeze ripe fruit, such as bananas or pineapple, simply peel or slice off the skin, cut into chunks and store in a sealed container in the freezer. I keep a variety of frozen fruit in our freezer including mango, mixed berries, blueberries, raspberries, strawberries, pineapple (or mixed tropical fruits) and, of course, ripe bananas.

Fresh Vegetables

I visit our local farmers' market every Saturday morning to stock up on fresh organic, in-season produce for the week ahead. I always purchase an abundance of dark leafy, vital greens, including kale, spinach, lettuce, rocket, sprouts and microgreens. Dark leafy greens are highly beneficial and provide a multitude of nutrients. And when eaten raw, greens are rich in protein and phytonutrients such as chlorophyll and flavonoids. They also include some of the essential nutrients of common concern when adopting a plant-based diet, including iron and calcium. Carrots, beetroot, potato, kūmara, cauliflower, broccoli, cabbage, red onion and garlic are some of the other weekly staples I like to have on hand. Although I enjoy spontaneous creativity when it comes to preparing good food, I also believe that a little meal planning can make it easier to eat better. When you feel prepared, you are more likely to eat your fresh, vibrant vegetables before the compost does!

Fresh Herbs

Fresh herbs work wonders as natural green flavour boosters while hosting many essential nutrients. Did you know fresh parsley has extremely beneficial health properties? The superfood herb has a highly alkalising effect in our body (similar to a lemon) along with being rich in vitamin C and antioxidants. Here are the herbs I commonly include in the majority of my recipes, especially in a good salad.

- Basil
- Chives
- Coriander
- Dill
- Makrut lime leaves (Kaffir)
- Mint
- Lemon grass stalks
- Parsley
- Thyme
- Rosemary

Dried Fruits and Natural Sweeteners

Natural sweeteners are excellent items to have on hand for snacks, smoothies, dressings and raw treats or to scatter over a salad to add a chewy

bite. They're an awesome sweet addition without the overload of refined sugar, such as white sugar, brown sugar, golden syrup and artificial maple syrup. Speaking of maple syrup, always purchase the 100 per cent pure version without any additives or artificial sweeteners. When purchasing dried fruit, look for sulphur- and preservative-free options.

- Apricots
- Coconut (desiccated, shredded or flakes/chips)
- Coconut sugar
- Cranberries
- Dates
- Figs
- Medjool dates
- Pure maple syrup (or brown rice syrup or coconut nectar)
- Raisins
- Sultanas

Nuts and Seeds

I usually have an array of glass jars full of nuts and seeds, which are a great source of vital nutrients including protein and healthy fats. They also work as an excellent, creamy base in many recipes such as smoothies, dressings, dips and raw treats. In our home, we routinely use cashews and hempseeds in dressings, sauces, smoothies and salads. Bulk bins can be a great way to shop for a variety of commonly used nuts and seeds, including the following items I regularly use in my home.

- Almonds (whole and sliced)
- Cashew nuts
- Chia seeds
- Flaxseeds
- Hempseeds (hemp hearts)
- Pecans
- Pine nuts
- Pumpkin seeds
- Sesame seeds (black and white)
- Sunflower seeds
- Walnuts

Dried Herbs and Spices

Every well-stocked kitchen will feature a wide variety of dried herbs and spices to liven up any dish and create a diverse range of popular cuisines. These are the herbs and spices I use in most of my recipes and always have on hand.

- Allspice
- Pepper (black peppercorns, cracked pepper and ground white pepper)
- Cardamom (ground and pods)
- Cayenne pepper
- Chilli flakes
- Chinese five spice
- Chipotle (ground)
- Cinnamon (ground)
- Cloves (ground)
- Coriander (ground and seeds)

- Cumin (ground and seeds)
- Curry powder (mild, yellow)
- Garam masala
- Garlic powder
- Ginger (ground)
- Mixed herbs
- Mixed spice
- Nutmeg
- Onion powder
- Oregano
- Paprika (smoked and sweet)
- Rosemary
- Sea salt (Himalayan)
- Sumac
- Thyme
- Turmeric (ground)

Gluten-free Wholegrains

Loaded with essential nutrients and often used as a substantial salad base, gluten-free wholegrains are a fabulous textural component that feature in many of my recipes. So, what exactly is a wholegrain? A wholegrain is a cereal grain that still contains the endosperm, germ and bran of the grain. Unlike processed grains such as white rice, wholegrains contain many essential nutrients, including fibre, protein, iron, zinc, B vitamins and magnesium. Below are my favourite gluten-free wholegrains. These provide a nutritious, hearty element to many recipes, including salads, baking and breakfast cereals, and are also fabulous served as a wholesome side. I also purchase these in the form of pasta, such as penne and spaghetti.

- Buckwheat
- Millet
- Quinoa (white, red and black)
- Rice (brown, black and red)
- Sorghum

Beans and Legumes (canned and/or dried)

Beans and legumes are other handy staples that add a protein and fibre component to bulk up any dish, including salads, tacos, nachos and plant-based bolognese. With their soft texture and neutral flavour profile, chickpeas, in particular, are a versatile ingredient I repeatedly use in my recipes. When purchasing canned beans and legumes, I always choose the organic options without stabilisers and extra additives. If you choose to buy these dried and cook your own, keep in mind they will need to be soaked prior to cooking. Below are beans and legumes commonly welcomed into my pantry.

- Black beans
- Brown lentils
- Cannellini beans
- Chickpeas
- Green lentils (dried)
- Kidney beans
- Red lentils (dried)

Gluten-free Flours

I choose to avoid gluten as I feel more energised without it, and it's much gentler on my digestive health. There are many gluten-free flours available (you can also make your own by grinding nuts or grains in your food processor), but I tend to keep it simple and stick to a small selection. While gluten-free flours are a wonderful alternative to standard wheat-based flours, they don't always provide quite the same texture, so they can take some time and experimenting to get used to. These are the flours I commonly use in my sauces, baking and raw treats. They are widely available in most supermarkets and health food stores.

- Almond meal (ground almonds or almond flour)
- Buckwheat flour
- Chickpea (besan) flour
- Coconut flour

Flavour Boosters

These items will elevate dips, dressings, sauces, salads, pasta dishes and mains. When purchasing, look for additive- and preservative-free options.

- Capers
- Dijon mustard
- Nutritional yeast flakes
- Olives
- Sun-dried tomatoes (oil-free)
- Tamari
- White miso paste
- Wholegrain mustard

Other Pantry Staples

The following items come in handy time and time again. Once again, ensure you read the ingredients labels when purchasing and select the most natural options you can, without unnecessary additives and preservatives.

- Almond butter
- Apple cider vinegar
- Baking soda and powder
- Balsamic vinegar
- Asian vermicelli noodles
- Cacao powder and nibs
- Coconut cream/milk (canned)
- Coconut yoghurt
- Hulled tahini
- Jackfruit
- Oats (gluten-free) or brown rice flakes
- Organic coconut oil
- Organic olive oil or avocado oil
- Organic tofu
- Peanut butter
- Pure vanilla extract or vanilla bean paste
- Rice milk (or other plant milk)
- Rice wine vinegar
- Sesame oil
- Tomato passata
- Wholegrain pasta and spaghetti (quinoa, rice, sorghum)

Commonly Used Ingredients

I designed the recipes in this book around a core group of staple ingredients. This way, you will become familiar with these particular ingredients, and it will be easier and more cost-effective for you to recreate the majority of my recipes, and you'll have the confidence to tweak them to your own tastes. All of my recipes are plant-based, dairy-free, refined-sugar free and gluten-free, and on the next few pages, I'll talk about some of the staple ingredients I repeatedly use in a little more detail. I'll also explain a few of the less common unique items featured in this book, including banana blossom and rose harissa paste. Hopefully, this will give you a better understanding of how best to use these ingredients, and how to include them in a wide variety of wholefood and plant-based recipes. It might also inspire you to get creative with any in-season produce you have on hand.

Banana blossom

Similar to jackfruit, the banana blossom is a fleshy, purple-skinned flower, which grows at the end of a banana cluster. Traditionally used in South-East Asian and Indian cooking, it's now widely popular as a vegan substitute for fish due to its flaky, chunky texture. I feature this neutral-flavoured blossom in my creamy and delicious Banana Blossom, Leek and Kūmara Crustless Pie with Cheesy Rosemary Crumble (page 152). Canned banana blossom is available in most supermarkets.

Cashew nuts

Raw, unsalted cashews are a key ingredient in many plant-based dips, dressings, sauces and raw treats as they have a mild flavour and a creamy, silky texture when blended. They often need to be soaked prior to blending so they soften (see Recipe Notes page 42), so keep this in mind when planning a recipe. Cashews are high in magnesium, making them a great snack or crunchy salad addition.

Chia seeds

Chia seeds are a fantastic pantry staple. They are loaded with nutrients such as essential amino acids, omega-3 fatty acids and fibre. They also work wonders as an egg replacement because when chia seeds are combined with liquid, they become gelatinous, making them a perfect binder in many recipes. Ground flaxseeds (linseeds) also serve the same purpose; they are another great substitute for eggs.

Hempseeds

My pantry is always stocked with hempseeds and thankfully, they are widely available in most supermarkets. Derived from the *Cannabis sativa* plant, hempseeds are the true essence of a superfood. Although they are the same species as the cannabis plant, they are a different variety and only contain minute traces of THC (the psychoactive component of cannabis). Hempseeds are highly nutritious with an earthy, nutty flavour. They play an important role in a plant-based diet because their versatility and creaminess mean you can add them to the majority of your meals, from smoothies to salads, desserts to plant milks. Hempseeds are also a great source of complete protein as they contain all nine essential amino acids, as well as vitamin E, phosphorus, potassium, sodium, magnesium, sulphur, calcium, iron and zinc.

Jackfruit

Jackfruit is an incredibly versatile addition to many plant-based salads and mains. The jack tree is a tropical fruit tree that originates from southwest India. The fruit it bears is large and oval with edible fibrous flesh, seeds and pods. Jackfruit is really popular in plant-based cooking due to the pulled-pork-like texture it has when cooked. Jackfruit is high in fibre, rich in vitamins B and C, as well as potassium, and works wonders as a marinated addition to tacos, nachos, burgers and curries. You can find canned young jackfruit in most supermarkets.

Medjool dates

Medjool dates are naturally super-sweet with a caramel-like flavour. They are also highly alkalising and nutritious. People often get confused about the difference between medjool dates and regular dates. Medjool dates are a soft, plump and chewy fresh fruit, whereas regular dates (commonly called deglet noor) are dried and smaller, with firmer flesh. Medjool dates are fantastic in raw vegan slices and baking as they're big and sticky, which really helps to bind ingredients and create a soft, chewy textural component. Dates in general are one of my favourite go-to wholesome snacks, not to mention the perfect addition to sweeten smoothies, dressings and raw treats. They can also be blended into a date syrup, which is a natural liquid sweetener.

Nutritional yeast flakes

Nutritional yeast is an absolute game-changer in plant-based cooking because it adds a savoury, cheesy flavour to almost any dish. I commonly blend these super-fine flakes into sauces and dressings or sprinkle them over pasta dishes, soups, pizzas and patties. Nutritional yeast, fortified with vitamin B12, is a deactivated yeast, so it will not rise or bubble the way brewer's yeast or baker's yeast does.

Pure maple syrup

Naturally derived from the sap of maple trees, maple syrup is one of my favourite unrefined sweeteners, and the one I repeatedly use in my recipes. It provides a subtle sweetness to almost any dish. I like to include it in my smoothies, salad dressings, curries, hot dishes and raw treats. When purchasing, always read the label to ensure the bottle is 100 per cent pure maple syrup, without any additives, sweeteners or preservatives. Other commonly used unrefined sweeteners include coconut sugar, agave nectar, brown rice syrup and date syrup.

Raw cacao powder

Raw cacao is the unprocessed version of cocoa; it's the ground-down cacao bean so it's still packed with antioxidants, vitamins and minerals. You'll find cacao powder in many of my raw treat recipes – I love using it to create decadent, chocolatey sweets.

Rose harissa paste

Complementing many dishes, dips and dressings, harissa is a wonderful North African spice paste that you can make at home or find easily in stores. Throughout *Simple Wholefoods*, I have chosen to use a natural rose harissa paste, which is a sweet, mild paste with the beautiful addition of rose petals. Rose harissa paste is available in most health food, international or Mediterranean food stores. You can also order it online.

Tahini

Tahini is a sesame paste made from toasted white or black sesame seeds. It is available 'hulled' or 'unhulled'. Hulled tahini means the outer shell of the sesame seed has been removed before grinding; it tends to be lighter in colour and has a creamier taste. Unhulled tahini is made from whole sesame seeds. It is darker and has a slightly more bitter flavour than hulled tahini. I prefer hulled tahini. It makes a fantastic creamy addition to many of my dips and dressings.

Tamari
Tamari, a wheat-free fermented soy sauce, works wonders when it comes to adding a rich, savoury and salty flavour. For a soy-free alternative, you can substitute coconut aminos. Coconut aminos is made from the fermented sap of the coconut palm. It has a similar salty flavour to tamari, although it's not quite as strong.

Vinegars
Apple cider vinegar is a key ingredient I use in dips and dressings or when I want to add a sweet, tangy vibe to a salad. It's also great for baking, as it helps to make a batter light and fluffy. Rice vinegar and balsamic vinegar are the other kinds of vinegar I commonly use in marinades, dressings, salads, traybakes or Asian-inspired recipes. When purchasing, try to choose products without unnecessary additives or preservatives in them.

White miso paste
Like tamari, white miso paste is made from fermented soy beans, and it has a similar flavour, but is much sweeter and thicker. You can also get brown rice miso paste, which is made from soy beans fermented with brown rice. White miso paste makes a fabulous, slightly salty, sweet and creamy addition to many dishes. It's especially good for enhancing the flavours of your favourite dressings, hot pots, soups, pasta dishes and pies. Good-quality white miso paste is available at some supermarkets and most health food stores.

Wholefood, Plant-based Swaps

There is almost always a healthier wholefood or plant-based alternative for all your everyday foods. Making quick, wholesome plant-based swaps for commonly used ingredients gets easier with practise. The suggestions below may not be quite the same as the ones you are trying to substitute, but they serve a similar purpose. Below are my favourite common swaps.

Eggs	Chia seeds Flaxseed Scrambled tofu Smashed chickpeas	To make a chia or flax 'egg' to use as a binding agent in a recipe, such as baking, combine 1 tablespoon chia seeds or ground flaxseed per 3 tablespoons of water. Let the mixture sit for 5–10 minutes to thicken and form a gel. Scrambled tofu or smashed chickpeas are a fabulous swap for scrambled eggs. Try the quick and tasty recipe on page 166.
Processed sugar	Pure maple syrup Coconut sugar Agave syrup Coconut nectar Brown rice syrup Medjool dates	Unrefined, natural sweeteners make excellent swaps for white and brown sugar. Pure maple syrup is my favourite and the one I most commonly use in my recipes.
Dairy milk	Almond milk Hemp milk Oat milk Rice milk	The creamiest plant-based milk has to be oat milk, but we use rice milk or hemp milk in our home.
Dairy yoghurt/cream	Coconut yoghurt Coconut cream	These items are fabulous alternatives for dairy yoghurts in curries, dips, dressings, baking and smoothies. You will barely notice the difference.
Cheese	Nutritional yeast flakes	Nutritional yeast flakes are wonderful in any dish that would usually include cheese, from pasta to pizzas and creamy sauces. Try my parmesan-like Cheesy Rosemary Crumble (page 152).

SIMPLE WHOLEFOODS

Ice cream	Frozen bananas and other frozen fruit	When blended with very little liquid, frozen bananas create the creamiest, ice-cream-like consistency. To create a diversity of flavours, add other frozen fruit.
Chocolate/cocoa powder	Raw cacao powder	I use raw cacao powder to create chocolatey treats or smoothies. There are plentiful options in the Raw Treats chapter (page 260).
Processed bread and crackers	Cabbage, lettuce, collard or spinach leaves Rice paper wraps	I use leafy greens as a lighter, healthier alternative to processed bread and crackers. Rice paper wraps work fabulously for eating the rainbow in raw vegetables.
Meat	Mushrooms Avocado Jackfruit Cauliflower Banana blossom Coconut Tofu Beans/legumes Walnuts	All of these items can be marinated to create a delicious alternative to meat. Beans/legumes, tofu and walnuts are a great source of protein, too.
Processed grains such as white rice and pasta	Brown rice Quinoa Buckwheat Sorghum Millet Spiralised zucchini, carrot, cucumber and butternut squash	Gluten-free pasta options are widely available, such as brown rice, quinoa, sorghum or pulse pasta. Spiralise zucchini, carrot or cucumber to create fantastic, fully raw noodles. Butternut squash can also be spiralised and cooked (along with carrots and zucchini) for warm dishes.

Essential Kitchen Tools

To create the majority of the recipes in this book, there are a few kitchen essentials you will need. These are the items I use in my kitchen time and time again to make wholesome eating as easy and efficient as possible.

High-powered blender

Investing in a good blender was essential for our family. We use a blender every single day to create nourishing smoothies and wholesome salad dressings. It really is a vital health tool I simply cannot live without. The blender we use, and the one I highly recommend, is a Vitamix. They are powerful, efficient, high-speed blenders that will allow you to easily create a variety of plant-based foods, including smoothies, smoothie bowls, soups, dips and dressings. If a Vitamix is out of your price range, I suggest doing some research and purchasing the most powerful blender that fits your budget. Or perhaps you could look into purchasing a secondhand Vitamix; in my opinion, they are definitely worth the investment.

Food processor

A high-quality food processor is another item I use regularly in my kitchen. Although they can be expensive, I can assure you they truly do make a world of difference in the kitchen. Once again, in my opinion, they are definitely worth the investment. The beauty of these machines is that they make it so easy to make a variety of healthful food, from bliss balls and raw slices to dressings, dips, hummus and pesto. They are also fantastic for grating and cutting produce, which can save you a lot of time in the kitchen.

There is a substantial difference between a blender and a food processor. Blenders require liquid to run, they have short blades and a very powerful motor as they work mostly with liquids (this is why they are also called liquidisers). In contrast, food processors are mostly for prepping solid foods, hence they have longer blades and come with many different attachments. I use my blender more often than my food processor, but I highly recommend having both items, as they serve very different purposes and are both incredibly useful when following a wholesome, plant-based lifestyle.

Large oven tray

If you don't have an extra-large oven tray already, I recommend investing in one to create a variety of delicious traybake meals. I include a few traybake recipes throughout this book and we'll chat more about these easy, all-in-one meals on page 132.

Recipe Notes

Oil
Generally, I use very little oil when cooking; I tend to use a splash of water to stir-fry my vegetables. When frying or baking vegetables, feel free to replace the extra virgin olive oil (or avocado oil) in the recipe with a splash of water, or use more or less oil to suit your individual preferences. Any oil in the majority of my dips and dressings can be replaced with water, although please keep in mind, the outcome and consistency will differ from the original recipe. Aside from this, sesame oil is used to add flavour and coconut oil is required for many, if not most, of my Raw Treats (page 260).

Salt
Feel free to omit or adjust the salt quantities to suit your palate. Himalayan salt is my personal preference.

Soaking nuts and seeds
For some of my dressing recipes, cashews or sunflower seeds will need to be presoaked. Soaking nuts and seeds softens them, making them easier to blend to a smooth and creamy texture. Also, when nuts and seeds are soaked, it decreases the antinutrients (such as phytate or phytic acid) that block our body's ability to absorb nutrients. To soak, simply place the nuts or seeds into a bowl, cover with water and leave for about eight hours. Drain and rinse before using. For a much faster preparation time, add them to a bowl of just-boiled water and soak for about an hour prior to using – this is what I usually do.

Dates
Unless stated otherwise, I use medjool dates in my recipes as they are generally larger, juicer and stickier than dried dates, and I find they work best if I'm going to be processing a large quantity. I will often remove them from the fridge 15 minutes prior to using so they blend a little easier. Dried dates are much cheaper, although they are generally smaller and firmer. If you would like to use dried dates, simply soak them in warm water for about 15 minutes, or until they have softened. Drain and squeeze out any excess water prior to using.

Curry powder
I use a mild yellow curry powder in my recipes because I find it works best and is less dominant in my recipes. Curry powder varies in strength, flavour and heat so keep this in mind when purchasing and cooking and adjust quantities accordingly to suit your taste.

SMOOTHIES

Smoothies are essential to life in our home, and in many ways they're a fundamental part of a wholesome, plant-based lifestyle. We routinely begin our mornings by drinking an energy-boosting blend of alkalising fruits. Given that smoothies take only a few minutes to prepare, followed by very little kitchen clean-up, I simply cannot think of an easier way to include a substantial amount of nutrition and hydration into your daily routine. In our home, we enjoy smoothies throughout the day, be it for breakfast or a mid-morning snack, for on-the-go fuel pre- and post-surf, with lunches or for dessert. Smoothies are also the perfect way to sneak a bunch of raw nutrients into small children. I'm forever concocting large jugs of delightful flavours, especially during the warmer months but equally, we'll enjoy a healthful smoothie nestled next to the fire throughout the chilly New Zealand winters. If you're looking to build lifelong healthy habits for you and your family and want to find ways to include more fruit and wholefoods in your daily routine, you best begin blending!

Smoothie Perfection

The following fruity recipes are a selection of my current favourite combinations. They are designed to serve one, but the quantities can easily be doubled for a larger serving. Before you begin blending, you might like to read the helpful notes below to ensure your smoothies are perfection.

Only use ripe, spotted bananas

First rule of thumb: *always* use ripe, spotty bananas as they will create a sweeter and creamier blend. Unripe or yellow/greenish bananas will majorly affect the outcome of your smoothie by creating a bland, unsweet flavour and chalky texture. Did you know that bananas are one of the only fruits that increase in nutritional value and sugar content (good sugar) after they have been picked unripe? For a thicker consistency to your smoothies, or to create a smoothie bowl, always use frozen bananas. To freeze, simply peel the banana, but *only* when ripe and spotty, then cut into chunks and place in a sealed container in the freezer. I always have a good supply of bananas on hand, both fresh and frozen, as they are used as the creamy base in most of my smoothies.

Use a high-powered blender

You will need a good, high-powered blender, such as a Vitamix, to create an ultra-smooth, creamy blend and to achieve a thicker, ice-cream-like consistency in a smoothie bowl. A good food processor also works well for smoothie bowls. (I go into these tools in a little more detail on page 41).

Choose your consistency

As I already mentioned, for a thicker smoothie consistency, use frozen bananas as opposed to fresh bananas. The only difference between a smoothie and a smoothie bowl is the consistency: smoothies include a larger quantity of liquid, while a smoothie bowl contains frozen fruit and as little liquid as possible to achieve the thick and creamy, ice-cream-like swirl. Therefore, any of the smoothie recipes on the following pages can easily be adapted to be a delicious smoothie bowl by simply using frozen fruit (including bananas) and less liquid. You may also want to double the quantities for a larger batch and vice versa for the smoothie bowl recipes – simply add more liquid to create a drinkable smoothie.

Add hempseeds

Hempseeds (hemp hearts) are my secret smoothie weapon. Generally, I only use water or coconut water as the liquid base for my smoothies, as opposed to plant milks. However, I almost always add hempseeds – about 2 tablespoons per serving. This is because when hempseeds are combined

with water in your smoothie, they help it to morph into the creamiest, yoghurt-like blend. Not to mention, the health benefits of hempseeds are extraordinary. They are a great source of complete protein as they contain all nine essential amino acids, as well as vitamin E, phosphorus, potassium, sodium, magnesium, sulphur, calcium, iron and zinc – that's a stellar list of beneficial nutrients!

Extra sweeteners

I enjoy my smoothies quite sweet, but feel free to adjust the ingredient quantities to suit your palate. I use pitted medjool dates or pure maple syrup to add extra sweetness to my smoothies. I also use coconut water for a sweeter blend, but you can replace that with filtered water if you prefer. If your bananas are ripe enough, you will need to add very little, if any, extra sweetener.

Optional superfood additions

Hempseeds aside, I usually keep my smoothies simple and fruit-based, but feel free to include any nutritional extras to bulk up your smoothies. Some easily disguisable options include chia seeds, ground or whole almonds and flaxseeds (linseeds), natural protein powders, spirulina, spinach, cacao powder or cacao nibs.

SERVES 1

DAILY GREENS SMOOTHIE

1 large very ripe banana, fresh or frozen
1 cup diced pineapple, fresh or frozen
1 cup fresh spinach leaves
½ cup diced frozen mango
2 tablespoons hempseeds
1–2 pitted medjool dates, or 1 teaspoon pure maple syrup
½ teaspoon finely grated fresh ginger
1 cup coconut water
small handful ice (optional)

The beautiful, fruity flavours of this smoothie make it an easy way to get more greens into your body. I prefer to use spinach for the green vegetable component in my fruit smoothies, as opposed to other dark, leafy greens. This is because the fibre content of spinach is much less dense than that of kale, collards and chard. This means that when spinach is blended with fruit, it will likely be digested at a similar rate, and therefore you will receive the maximum nutrients from your green smoothie. Be sure to add this hydrating recipe to your morning routine.

Place all the ingredients in a blender and blend on high speed for about 30 seconds, or until smooth. Pour into a large glass or jar and enjoy.

SERVES 1

VITAMIN BOOST GREEN SMOOTHIE

1 large very ripe banana, fresh or frozen
2 oranges, peeled
1 apple, cored
juice ½ lemon
handful baby spinach leaves
2 large pitted medjool dates
1 cup coconut water
hint finely grated fresh ginger
handful ice

Green smoothies are wonderful vehicles for a multitude of essential nutrients, which overflow from a single serve. This vibrant green blend is made up of fresh winter fruits, including apples, oranges and lemons, that grow abundantly in many backyards here in New Zealand. If you're in need of a daily nutrient boost, this hydrating, wholesome smoothie is for you. Just remember to blend it with ice.

Place all the ingredients in a blender and blend on high speed for about 30 seconds, or until smooth. Pour into a large glass or jar and enjoy.

SERVES 1

MANGO LASSI

1 large very ripe banana
2 cups frozen mango
¼ cup coconut yoghurt
1 teaspoon pure maple syrup
1 cup coconut water
1 tablespoon hempseeds (optional)

When I was fifteen, my family and I spent an adventurous, sun-drenched month in one of my favourite tropical destinations: Bali. Fresh mango lassis – a beautiful blend of fresh fruit and yoghurt – featured on just about every menu and quickly became my go-to daily quencher. Here is my simple, wholesome, dairy-free version. It will cool your palate, boost your energy levels and likely leave you craving another glassful.

Place all the ingredients in a blender and blend on high speed for about 30 seconds, or until smooth. Pour into a large glass or jar and enjoy.

SERVES 1

TROPICAL STRAWBERRY SMOOTHIE

1 large very ripe banana, fresh or frozen
1 cup frozen strawberries
½ cup diced frozen mango
½ cup diced pineapple
1 cup coconut water
1–2 pitted medjool dates, or 1 teaspoon pure maple syrup

This addictive blend is one of my go-to daily smoothies, and it's my son Eli's all-time favourite! We often enjoy the sweet, refreshing blend for breakfast, but it's equally good throughout the day. The specifically selected fruity ingredients work amazingly together to create the perfect blend of tropical goodness, with a delightful twist of strawberries. I definitely recommend pouring this mixture into ice-block moulds – just double or triple the quantities.

Place all the ingredients in a blender and blend on high speed for about 30 seconds, or until smooth. Pour into a large glass or jar and enjoy.

SERVES 1

MANGO, LIME AND RASPBERRY SMOOTHIE

1 large very ripe banana, fresh or frozen
1 cup diced frozen mango
½ cup frozen raspberries
juice ½ lime
1 cup coconut water
2 tablespoons hempseeds
2 pitted medjool dates or 1 teaspoon pure maple syrup

Mango and raspberry is a dreamy combo. This zesty variation is an old favourite I became obsessed with a few years ago. I would enjoy it almost every day during the warm summer months – blissful! The hint of lime juice provides a refreshing mouthful combined with the vibrant fruit but if you don't have a ripe lime on hand, it is equally as good without. I always add hempseeds for the added creaminess and nutritional benefits.

Place all the ingredients in a blender and blend on high speed for about 30 seconds, or until smooth. Pour into a large glass or jar and enjoy.

SERVES 1

ANTIOXIDANT BLUEBERRY SMOOTHIE

1 large very ripe banana, fresh or frozen
1 cup frozen blueberries
2 tablespoons hempseeds
½ cup pure grape juice (see recipe intro)
½ cup coconut water
1–2 pitted medjool dates, or 1 teaspoon pure maple syrup

One-hundred per cent pure grape juice (usually found in health food stores, liquor stores or at a winery; not the grape juice sold in supermarkets) is a powerful detoxifying drink. If you can get hold of it, definitely add it to this antioxidant-rich blend. It creates the sweetest, most delicious drink that is full of incredible health benefits and impossible not to love. If you don't have grape juice to hand, just use coconut water – the smoothie will still be amazing and super healthy.

Place all the ingredients in a blender and blend on high speed for about 30 seconds, or until smooth. Pour into a large glass or jar and enjoy.

WHOLESOME OREO SMOOTHIE

SERVES 1

With minimal ingredients, this gorgeous smoothie creates a satisfyingly wholesome treat. The addition of the cacao nibs provides a textural and chocolatey Oreo-like crunch with each mouthful. Last summer, I would make this with my boys all the time, and sometimes we would use fresh bananas and loads of ice (instead of using frozen bananas) to create a sorbet-style smoothie.

Place the bananas, hempseeds, maple syrup, coconut water and half of the cacao nibs in a blender and blend on high speed for about 30 seconds, or until smooth. Add the remaining cacao nibs and blend again for about 5 seconds. Pour into a large glass or jar and enjoy.

2 large very ripe frozen bananas
3 tablespoons hempseeds
1 teaspoon pure maple syrup
1 cup coconut water
2½ tablespoons cacao nibs

MILO'S PB AND CHOC SMOOTHIE

SERVES 1

This luscious, thickshake-style smoothie is extra special because it was created by one of my beautiful boys, Milo. He went through a phase of whizzing one up for him and his big bro, Eli, every evening after dinner. I tried it one day and instantly knew it had a place in this book. Milo did all of the creating and measuring, and I got to be the lucky observer and tester. Trust me, this one's a real goodie for all ages.

Place all the ingredients in a blender and blend on high speed for about 30 seconds, or until smooth. Pour into a large glass or jar and enjoy.

2 large very ripe frozen bananas
1 tablespoon smooth peanut butter
2 teaspoons cacao powder
2 teaspoons pure maple syrup
1 cup rice milk or other plant milk

SERVES 2–3

PIÑA COLADA SMOOTHIE BOWL

2 large very ripe frozen bananas
2 cups frozen pineapple (see recipe intro)
2 tablespoons pure maple syrup
½ cup canned coconut milk
3 tablespoons shredded coconut
¼ cup coconut water
1 teaspoon lime or lemon zest

TOPPINGS PER BOWL
1 sliced banana
½ cup diced fresh pineapple
1 tablespoon shredded coconut, lightly toasted (optional but recommended)
½ teaspoon hempseeds
granola (page 210, or store-bought) (optional)

Celebrating sweet pineapple and earthy coconut, this utterly refreshing bowl will cool your tastebuds and take you straight to the tropics. The key to this recipe is ensuring your pineapple is really ripe and sweet. Simply freeze the pineapple the night before to create this quick, nutritious breakfast, lunch or snack with an irresistible combination of creamy and juicy flavours.

Place all the ingredients in a high-powered blender or food processor and let sit for about 5 minutes, to allow the fruit to slightly soften.

Start by blending on a low speed. Use a blending stick to assist with moving the fruit (if using a blender), then slowly increase to a high speed as it begins to easily blend. You will probably need to stop the blender, mix and blend again, until you get a thick, creamy swirl.

Divide between serving bowls and arrange the toppings on each portion. Serve immediately.

SERVES 2–3

MIXED BERRY SMOOTHIE BOWL WITH ALMOND BUTTER AND GRANOLA

2 cups frozen mixed berries
3 large very ripe frozen bananas
½–¾ cup coconut water
¼ cup coconut cream (optional) (see tip)

TOPPINGS PER BOWL
1 cup chopped fresh fruit (bananas, berries)
⅓ cup granola (page 210, or store-bought)
1 tablespoon almond butter (optional)

Refuel and refresh with this dreamy berry bowl; one your body will thank you for. The thick, gorgeous consistency that is generously dressed in fruity toppings and a hearty sprinkle of granola, creates a light, nourishing meal that will easily satisfy you at any time of the day. Feel free to mix up the berries with whatever you have on hand – frozen strawberries alone are also divine.

Place all the ingredients in a high-powered blender or food processor and let sit for about 5 minutes, to allow the fruit to slightly soften.

Start by blending on a low speed. Use a blending stick to assist with moving the fruit (if using a blender), then slowly increase to a high speed as it begins to easily blend. You will probably need to stop the blender, mix and blend again, until you get a thick, creamy swirl.

Divide between serving bowls and arrange the toppings on each portion. Serve immediately.

Tip: *If you're opening a new can of coconut cream, scoop the thick layer off the top and use that in this recipe to dial up the creaminess factor.*

SERVES 2

MY FAMOUS CHOCOLATE SMOOTHIE BOWL

4 large very ripe frozen bananas
2 tablespoons hempseeds
2 tablespoons cacao powder
1 tablespoon pure maple syrup
¼ cup coconut cream (use thick top layer)
½ cup coconut water
½ teaspoon pure vanilla

TOPPINGS PER BOWL
2 fresh strawberries, sliced
1 small banana, sliced
1 teaspoon cacao nibs
1 tablespoon coconut flakes (coconut chips)
1 teaspoon peanut butter (optional)

Dessert for breakfast, anyone? A popular household favourite, this admirable, wholesome swirl is highly renowned for its addictive natural creaminess and sweet, chocolatey vibes that will have you craving it time and again. My children adore my chocolate smoothies, especially when they're served in these nourishing, drool-worthy bowls.

Place all the ingredients in a high-powered blender or food processor and let sit for about 5 minutes, to allow the bananas to slightly soften.

Start by blending on a low speed. Use a blending stick to assist with moving the bananas (if using a blender), then slowly increase to a high speed as the fruit begins to easily blend. You will probably need to stop the blender, mix and blend again, until you get a thick, creamy swirl.

Divide between serving bowls and arrange the toppings on each portion. Serve immediately.

SUPER SALADS

SUPER SALADS

The Hearty Salads chapter in *Raw & Free*, was particularly popular, so here we are again, with a delicious and thoughtfully curated selection of salads full of wholefood goodness to expand your weekly menu.

   A fully loaded salad is one of the easiest ways to include an abundance of colourful and nutritious ingredients on one plate, and I'm not just talking about a salad of traditional garden green variety – you know the type: fresh lettuce with a light scattering of cherry tomatoes and red onion. I've spent years ordering the only salad options available at restaurants around the globe only to be handed this particular combo, so don't worry, I get it. But, oh, how times have changed! The modern-day salad embraces a much wider variety of wholefoods and is powered by layers upon layers in unique combinations, pronounced flavours and contrasting textures, resulting in a delicious main or wholesome side that leaves you feeling fulfilled, energised and beyond satisfied. How exactly do you create a salad like this? There really are no rules; your imagination is the limit. You can make it as simple or as complex as you like, but there is definitely a rhythm I tend to follow. This also applies when making Buddha bowls, which are creative bowlfuls of wholefoods. So, let's break that rhythm down over the following page.

Layers are the key to building a substantial salad or Buddha bowl

A satisfying salad is all about building layers, and sometimes this can be as simple as layering three or four different ingredients with a delicious dressing — a little effort with a big impact. A traybake (see page 132) is another great way to build a salad; it works as a fabulous base and only requires one simple tray. With the following steps in mind, try not to overcomplicate things. Use whatever ingredients you have on hand, including fresh, in-season produce.

1. **Choose a base:** A base ingredient can be a gluten-free wholegrain such as brown rice, quinoa, millet or buckwheat, and/or healthy carbohydrates such as kūmara (sweet potato) or potato, and/or proteins such as beans and legumes (chickpeas and lentils are my favourites). Roast cauliflower is another popular choice. I usually choose one or two of these options as a base for my salad or bowl.

2. **Add alkalising greens:** Next, add one (or a combination of) raw leafy greens. My favourites include fresh kale, spinach, cos lettuce, microgreens, mesclun and baby rocket leaves. I also like to include one or two fresh herbs such as parsley, dill, coriander, mint or basil to naturally enhance the flavour and nutrients.

3. **Include rainbow veggies:** Select a few raw (or cooked) veggies for a bit of colour, flavour, texture and nutrition. Great options include broccoli, carrot, beetroot, capsicum, sprouts, red onion, spring onion, edamame beans or veggie-like fruit such as jackfruit, avocado, tomato or cucumber.

4. **Work in dried herbs, spices or fruit:** Dried herbs and spices are great natural flavour boosters. My favourite dried herbs to use in a salad include thyme and rosemary, and I often choose spices depending on my chosen cuisine: turmeric and cumin if I'm going for an Indian meal, paprika and chilli if I'm leaning towards Mexican. Adding a chewy burst of natural sweetness can really boost your salad, too. I love throwing in some raisins, sultanas, currants, cranberries, apricots or dates. All of the above are optional extras.

5. **Add healthy fats:** A scattering of healthy fats or extra protein in the form of nuts and seeds adds another key texture to a hearty salad or Buddha bowl. They aren't essential, but they are great additions, especially if you want to increase the nutrients or bulk up your salad with an earthy crunch. Almonds, cashews, walnuts, pecans, pistachios, sesame seeds, pine nuts and hempseeds are all on rotation at my house. A creamy avocado is also a star staple healthy fat in any plant-based meal.

6. **Make a game-changing dressing:** A final drizzle (and this step is crucial) of an epic homemade dressing is what transforms a salad or Buddha bowl and takes it to a whole new level. This is why I created the Dips and Dressings chapter (see page 232); it's a tool to help you really step up your salad and Buddha bowl game! There is also a variety of seriously delicious dressings throughout this chapter and the next one, Everyday Mains.

Fully Raw

If you wish to construct a fully raw salad or bowl, simply skip the first step of the previous page (choosing a grain, legume or cooked vegetable). Personally, I like to keep the majority of the veggies in my salads in their raw and natural state, and I encourage you to do the same. I believe this is where our focus should flow: obtaining the many health benefits of raw, living food where possible. Most raw plants are far superior to cooked plants when it comes to easily absorbed nutrients, such as simple amino acids, iron, and many vitamins and minerals. When heat is applied, especially at high temperatures, nutrients rapidly decrease and the enzymes of the plant are destroyed, and this can change the way that plant is metabolised by the body. I highly recommend looking into the power of eating raw, organic plants and making a conscious effort to include more of them into your daily routine. In my experience, a good plant-based salad or Buddha bowl with a healthy, homemade dressing is one of the simplest, most effective and delicious ways to eat the rainbow when it comes to raw veggies. There is an abundance of raw dressings on offer throughout this book to complement your vibrant creations and enhance your natural palate.

Easy Weekday Prepping

I hope this chapter inspires you to experiment at home, and start throwing together different combinations of wholefoods, raw plants and beautiful dressings to optimise your weekly nutrients in a fun and delicious way. The following salads are either revitalising as a wholesome side, or hearty and fulfilling enough to be served as a main meal. They can be refrigerated for at least three days, which allows for easy, make-ahead work lunches or wholesome dinners. With a little planning and preparation, it can be easier to eat wholesomely on those busy working weeks.

Another simple idea that I know works for many, is to prep certain food groups ahead of time. For example, throw a simple traybake of potato, kūmara and pumpkin together and prep a few cups of cooked wholegrains, such as quinoa or millet. If you're feeling proactive, whizz up an easy hummus or a delectable dressing (there are plenty of recipes to explore in this book, and they're all so easy!). All of these things can be prepped efficiently and then refrigerated in separate containers to create easy lunches or quick dinners during the week, alongside fresh greens and avocado. With minimal effort, you can easily compose a quick bowlful of nourishment. Using a variety of dressings and fresh produce means each bowl can be altered with new and exciting flavours.

SERVES 4 OR 6–8 AS A SIDE

LEMONY MISO MILLET, BROCCOLI AND EDAMAME SALAD

⅔ cup millet (or white quinoa)
1⅓ cups water
1 large head broccoli (about 550 g/1 lb 4 oz), cut into bite-sized florets
½ cup sliced almonds
1½ tablespoons black sesame seeds
1½ cups frozen edamame beans, thawed
2 spring onions, finely sliced

MISO DRESSING
¼ cup white miso paste
3 tablespoons lemon juice
1 tablespoon tamari
2½ tablespoons pure maple syrup

This wholesome salad comes together with ease and the ingredients mingle to create the perfect balance of flavours and textures. The broccoli is very lightly steamed (or blanched) to ensure it retains crunch and nutrients, while the lemony miso dressing contributes a subtle depth of zingy and salty flavours. I love the simplicity of this wholefood, super salad and find it works wonders as a packed lunch, light dinner or as a delicious side salad for a barbecue.

Place the millet and water in a saucepan, cover and bring to a boil. Reduce the heat and simmer for 10–12 minutes, or until the water has absorbed and the millet is soft and fluffy.

Bring a saucepan half-filled with water to a boil. Place the broccoli in a colander over the water, cover, and steam for about 5 minutes, or until the florets are just tender. Alternatively, blanch the florets.

Heat a small frying pan over medium–high heat. Add the sliced almonds and sesame seeds and toast for about 2 minutes, swirling the pan constantly to avoid burning.

For the Miso dressing, place all the ingredients in a bowl and whisk until smooth.

To serve, place all the salad ingredients into a large serving bowl. Add the dressing and toss gently to combine.

**SERVES 4 OR
6–8 AS A SIDE**

MOREISH MAPLE MUSTARD CRISPY POTATO, MESCLUN AND FRESH HERB SALAD

MAPLE MUSTARD POTATOES
5 large (about 900 g/2 lb) agria potatoes, cut into bite-sized cubes
¼ cup pure maple syrup
¼ cup wholegrain mustard
¼ cup olive or avocado oil
sea salt and cracked pepper, to taste

SALAD
2–3 handfuls mesclun leaves (or baby spinach or rocket leaves)
2 spring onions, finely sliced
handful fresh mint, roughly chopped
handful fresh parsley, roughly chopped
small handful fresh tarragon, finely chopped
1 bunch fresh chives, finely chopped
3 small radishes, finely sliced then cut into matchsticks
2 tablespoons capers, drained

You're going to love these drool-worthy potatoes; they're both indulgent and very moreish. This salad was an immediate winner with the whole family. I start by submerging soft, fluffy potatoes in a sweet mustard marinade, then I bake them to crispy perfection before tossing through fresh herbs, salty capers, sliced radishes and mesclun. Yum is an understatement. My children Eli and Milo also love eating these marinated potato bites as a delectable snack with a drizzle of Hemp Miso Aioli (page 252) or Creamy Dill Ranch Dressing (page 252).

Preheat the oven to 180°C (350°F) fan-bake. Line a large baking tray with baking paper.

For the Maple mustard potatoes, bring a saucepan half-filled with water to a boil. Place the potatoes in a colander over the water, cover, and steam for 15 minutes, or until just tender.

For the marinade, place the maple syrup, mustard and oil into a large bowl, season to taste and whisk to combine. Add the potatoes and gently toss them through the marinade, ensuring they are evenly coated. Transfer to the prepared tray and drizzle over any remaining marinade. Bake for 25–30 minutes, until golden and crispy. Let potatoes cool slightly.

To make the salad, place all the ingredients in a bowl, reserving some radish for garnish, and toss to combine.

To serve, transfer to a serving platter or bowl and top with the reserved radish.

HARISSA YOGHURT ROAST CAULIFLOWER, CHICKPEAS, ROCKET AND TOASTED ALMONDS

SERVES 4 OR 6–8 AS A SIDE

I could seriously eat this salad just about every day of the week; it's all kinds of wonderful and a definite favourite in the book! It requires minimal effort to put together and is always so popular. It has quickly become my go-to impressive salad for feeding guests and it's the perfect pick for a potluck dinner. Complementing many dishes, dips and dressings, harissa is a wonderful North African spice paste that can be homemade or easily found in stores. For this particular recipe, I've gone for a natural rose harissa paste – a sweet and mild paste with added rose petals.

Preheat the oven to 180°C (350°F) fan-bake. Line a large baking tray with baking paper.

Place the cauliflower florets and chickpeas on the prepared tray and spread out in a single layer. Sprinkle over the coriander and cumin seeds. Lightly drizzle with oil, if desired, and season to taste. Bake for about 25 minutes, until tender.

Heat a frying pan over medium heat. Add the almonds and cook, tossing frequently to avoid burning, for about 2 minutes, until toasted and fragrant.

For the Harissa yoghurt dressing, place all the ingredients in a bowl and mix to combine.

To make the salad, place the roasted cauliflower and chickpeas, almonds, rocket and spring onion in a large bowl and toss to combine. Add the dressing and gently mix through.

Transfer to a serving platter or bowl and serve.

Tip: *Store-bought harissa paste varies in strength and heat so keep this in mind and adjust accordingly when making this dressing. Rose harissa is a gorgeous variation I chose for this salad, however, any natural harissa paste will work. Rose harissa is available in most health food or Mediterranean food stores. You can also order it online.*

1 large head cauliflower, cut into florets, then finely sliced
400 g (14 oz) can chickpeas, drained and rinsed (or 1½ cups cooked chickpeas)
2 teaspoons coriander seeds
1 teaspoon cumin seeds
drizzle olive or avocado oil (optional)
sea salt and cracked pepper, to taste
¾ cup sliced almonds
2–3 handfuls rocket leaves (or baby spinach)
2 spring onions, finely sliced

HARISSA YOGHURT DRESSING
¾ cup coconut yoghurt
2 tablespoons lime juice
2 tablespoons mild rose harissa paste (see tip)
1 teaspoon pure maple syrup

PAD THAI VERMICELLI NOODLE SALAD

SERVES 2–3 OR 4 AS A SIDE

200 g (7 oz) pack brown rice vermicelli noodles (see tip) or pad Thai noodles
3 spring onions, finely sliced
1 red capsicum, finely sliced
1 large carrot, peeled and julienned
1 cup mung bean sprouts
large handful fresh coriander, roughly chopped, plus extra leaves to serve
bunch 1 chives, finely chopped
¼ cup unsalted peanuts, roughly chopped, plus extra to serve

PAD THAI DRESSING
⅓ cup almond butter
¼ cup lime juice
2 tablespoons tamari
2 tablespoons pure maple syrup
2 teaspoons sesame oil
1 clove garlic, crushed or finely grated
1 teaspoon finely grated fresh ginger

TO SERVE
lemon or lime wedges

Here's another goodie: a fresh take on the popular Brown Rice Asian Noodle Salad with Sesame Lime Dressing from my first cookbook. The creamy, sweet and tangy dressing boasts zingy Asian flavours and pairs perfectly with the raw veggies and vermicelli noodles to create a clean and nourishing lunch or light dinner. Prepping this flavourful rainbow salad couldn't be simpler and it's also a wonderful way to catch up on your raw veggie intake, as well as a great pick for little people.

Bring a large saucepan of water to a boil. Add the noodles and cook according to the packet instructions (usually about 4 minutes) until soft. Be careful not to overcook as the noodles can become too soft and mushy. Drain and rinse in cold water immediately to stop the noodles from cooking any further.

For the Pad Thai dressing, place all the ingredients in a bowl and whisk together until smooth.

To make the salad, place the noodles, spring onion, capsicum, carrot, sprouts, coriander, chives and peanuts in a large bowl. Pour over the dressing and toss to combine well.

Transfer the salad to a serving bowl. Scatter over the extra peanuts and coriander and serve with a squeeze of lemon or lime juice.

Tip: *I personally enjoy the fine texture of vermicelli noodles, but you can also use the traditional pad Thai rice noodles. To make this a fully raw salad, simply replace the vermicelli noodles with kelp noodles or spiralised zucchini noodles.*

CHIPOTLE MEXICAN BAKED JACKFRUIT AND BLACK BEAN SALAD WITH CORIANDER CREAM

SERVES 4 OR 6–8 AS A SIDE

I'm big on Mexican food and I'm a fan of any dish inspired by it. I love the fresh flavours and nourishing ingredients. You'll be delighted by the sheer simplicity of this must-try, versatile salad. The seasoned jackfruit and black beans are packed with punchy flavours, including a subtle hint of smoky chipotle, and it makes a fabulous meal when served over nachos, wraps and tacos. Be sure to add a few generous dollops of the delicious Coriander Cream (page 246) – a wholesome dressing I like to eat by the spoonful!

Preheat the oven to 180°C (350°F) fan-bake. Line a large baking tray with baking paper.

For the Jackfruit and black bean base, place all the ingredients in a bowl and gently toss to combine. Transfer the mixture to the prepared tray and spread out evenly. Bake, tossing once or twice during cooking, for about 20–25 minutes. Allow to cool slightly.

To make the salad, place the spinach leaves, basil, olives and red onion in a serving bowl. Add three-quarters of the Jackfruit and black bean base and gently toss through the salad. Squeeze the lemon juice over evenly.

To serve, top with the remaining Jackfruit and black beans then scatter over the extra sliced olives and coriander seeds. Add a few dollops of the Coriander Cream and serve any remaining dressing on the side.

JACKFRUIT AND BLACK BEAN BASE

2 x 400 g (14 oz) cans young jackfruit, drained, rinsed and broken into smaller pieces
400 g (14 oz) can black beans, drained and rinsed (or 1½ cups cooked black beans)
¼ cup coconut yoghurt (or thick coconut cream)
3 tablespoons pure maple syrup
2 tablespoons lime juice
1 tablespoon dried oregano
1½ teaspoons paprika
1 teaspoon garlic powder
1 teaspoon onion powder
1 teaspoon cumin seeds
½ teaspoon ground chipotle powder
½ teaspoon sea salt
¼ teaspoon smoked paprika

SALAD

about 3 large handfuls baby spinach leaves
handful fresh basil leaves, roughly chopped
⅓ cup pitted black olives, sliced, plus extra to serve
½ small red onion, finely sliced
1 small lemon, halved, or ½ a large lemon
1½ cups Coriander Cream (page 246)

TO SERVE (OPTIONAL)
coriander seeds

MOROCCAN CHERMOULA MILLET WITH ROAST EGGPLANT, CAPERS, FENNEL AND PINE NUTS

SERVES 4 OR 6–8 AS A SIDE

2 eggplants, cut lengthways into 1–2 cm (½–¾ in) batons
½ cup capers, drained, plus extra to serve
¼ cup pine nuts
¾ teaspoon fennel seeds
2 tablespoons sesame oil
1 cup millet (or quinoa)
2 cups water
1 tablespoon balsamic vinegar
¼ cup currants (optional)
1 cup Moroccan Chermoula (page 246)
2 handfuls baby spinach leaves
handful fresh mint leaves, plus extra leaves to serve

Looking for something a little different and a little wonderful, with a refreshing impact? This glorious Middle Eastern blend of fresh herbs and spices, earthy millet and a simple tray of four key ingredients – soft, juicy eggplant, crispy salted capers, pine nuts and aromatic fennel seeds – comes together to create the most delish, substantial salad. I asked Ricardo to be the final tester of this delightful dish one sunny afternoon. He tried a large mouthful, then another, and another until well over half the salad was gone. He looked up at me with a gleeful expression and announced, 'This is really good, don't change a thing'.

Preheat the oven to 180°C (350°F) fan-bake. Line a large baking tray with baking paper.

Arrange the eggplant on the prepared tray in a single layer. Sprinkle over the capers, pine nuts and fennel seeds, then drizzle over the sesame oil. Bake for 45–60 minutes, or until the eggplant is tender and slightly charred.

Place the millet and water in a saucepan, cover and bring to a boil. Reduce the heat and simmer for 10–12 minutes, or until the water has absorbed and the millet is soft and fluffy.

To make the salad, place the roasted eggplant, millet, vinegar and currants, if using, in a bowl. Add the chermoula and evenly toss through the salad.

To serve, arrange the spinach leaves and fresh mint on a serving plate. Spoon the eggplant mixture over the leaves and sprinkle over the extra capers and mint leaves.

SERVES 4 OR 6–8 AS A SIDE

GARLIC BROCCOLI, CHICKPEAS, RED CHILLI AND ROCKET WITH TURMERIC TAHINI YOGHURT

3 small heads of broccoli, cut into small florets
400 g (14 oz) can chickpeas, drained and rinsed (or 1½ cups cooked chickpeas)
8 cloves garlic, finely chopped
olive oil (optional)
sea salt and cracked pepper, to taste
¼ cup pine nuts
2 large handfuls baby rocket leaves
1–2 red chillies, finely sliced (deseed if desired)
1 avocado, stoned and sliced

TURMERIC TAHINI YOGHURT
⅓ cup coconut yoghurt
2 tablespoons hulled tahini
2 tablespoons lemon juice
1 tablespoon tamari
1 tablespoon pure maple syrup
½ teaspoon ground turmeric
½ teaspoon apple cider vinegar
½ teaspoon garlic powder
¼ teaspoon mild yellow curry powder

Overflowing with gorgeous flavours, colours and textural elements, this tasty, wholesome salad wins me over every time. I love the subtle spice from the finely sliced red chilli, the crunch from the toasted pine nuts and the simple, garlicky broccoli and chickpea traybake — all enriched by a vibrant, creamy dressing. Packing a punch of delicious flavours, this epic salad has to be one of my favourite picks when I'm asked to bring a dish for a potluck.

Preheat the oven to 180°C (350°F) fan-bake. Line a large baking tray with baking paper.

Place the broccoli, chickpeas and garlic on the prepared tray and spread out evenly. Lightly drizzle with olive oil, if using, and season to taste. Bake for 15–18 minutes, or until the broccoli is just tender and slightly charred.

Meanwhile, heat a frying pan over medium heat. Add the pine nuts and cook, tossing frequently to avoid burning, for about 2 minutes, until fragrant. Set aside.

For the Tumeric tahini yoghurt, place all of the ingredients in a small bowl and mix until smooth and creamy.

To serve, place all the ingredients in a large bowl reserving some chilli slices to garnish and gently toss to combine. Transfer to a serving plate and garnish with extra slices of chilli.

SERVES 4 OR 6–8 AS A SIDE

SPICED ROAST CAULIFLOWER, GREEN LENTILS AND TOASTED ALMONDS WITH SMOKY YOGHURT

SPICED CAULIFLOWER

1 head cauliflower, cut into florets, then thickly sliced
2 tablespoons olive oil
1 teaspoon ground cumin
1 teaspoon ground turmeric
1 teaspoon paprika
½ teaspoon onion powder
pinch cayenne pepper (optional)

LENTIL BASE

1 cup dried green lentils, rinsed
3 cups water
¾ cup sliced almonds
1½ cups finely sliced curly kale or cavolo nero leaves
1 cup roughly chopped fresh mint leaves, plus extra mint leaves to serve
2 tablespoons tamari
3 tablespoons lemon juice
1 tablespoon coriander seeds
1 tablespoon pure maple syrup
1 teaspoon sea salt

SMOKY YOGHURT DRESSING

½ cup coconut yoghurt
1 tablespoon lemon juice
2 teaspoons tamari
1 teaspoon pure maple syrup
½–¾ teaspoon smoked paprika
½ teaspoon garlic powder

I encourage you to be adventurous with roast cauliflower as it makes a wonderful, neutral salad base. Taste-wise, its subtle presence means the sky's the limit when it comes to the flavours you can add to it. I particularly love combining cauliflower with legumes, such as chickpeas and lentils, or gluten-free wholegrains, such as quinoa or millet, to create a solid salad base. I've chosen green lentils for this delicious salad, and yum, what a salad it is. The aromatic spiced cauliflower plays against the carefully curated lentil mixture, and it's beautifully finished with a generous drizzle of the flavoursome smoky yoghurt to conquer an outstanding, hearty salad.

Preheat the oven to 180°C (350°F) fan-bake. Line a large baking tray with baking paper.

For the Spiced cauliflower, place all the ingredients in a bowl and toss until the cauliflower is evenly coated in the spices. Transfer to the prepared tray and spread out in a single layer. Bake for about 25 minutes, or until cauliflower is tender.

For the Lentil base, place the lentils and water in a saucepan, cover, and bring to a boil. Reduce the heat and simmer for 20–25 minutes, until soft. Drain and set aside.

Heat a small frying pan over medium–high heat. Add the almonds and toast, swirling the pan almost constantly to avoid burning, for about 2 minutes or until fragrant.

For the Smoky yoghurt dressing place all the ingredients in a bowl and mix to combine.

To make the salad, put the kale, mint, tamari, lemon juice, coriander seeds, maple syrup and salt in a large bowl. Add the roasted cauliflower, lentils and most of the toasted almonds, then toss to combine.

To serve, transfer the salad to a serving plate and scatter over the reserved almonds, and the extra mint leaves. Drizzle over the smoky yoghurt. Serve any remaining dressing on the side.

**SERVES 4 OR
6–8 AS A SIDE**

BAKED YAM, CARAMELISED PECANS AND ROCKET WITH SWEET MUSTARD AND LEMON TAHINI

700 g (1 lb 9 oz) yams, halved lengthways
olive oil (optional)
sea salt and cracked pepper to taste
3 handfuls baby rocket leaves
handful microgreens
½ small red onion, finely sliced
1 cup Sweet Mustard and Lemon Tahini Dressing (page 249)

CARAMELISED PECANS
1 cup pecans
1 tablespoon balsamic vinegar
1 tablespoon pure maple syrup
1 teaspoon olive oil
few pinches sea salt

When I was gathering the mountain of ingredients required to shoot this book, I was stunned by a vibrant array of yams proudly displayed among the green produce. Later that day, I spoke to my wonderful photographer, Lottie Hedley, who had also been drawn to a display of brightly coloured yams. Randomly, she asked if I would be featuring them in any of my recipes. I took this as a sign and with the help of my superstar kitchen assistants (thanks Mum and Emma!), I excitedly created this delightful salad. The baked caramelised pecans are seriously divine. When that sweet and crunchy element is tossed through creamy baked yams and fresh baby rocket leaves, then matched like a dream with a sweet mustard dressing . . . Delish!

Preheat the oven to 180°C (350°F) fan-bake. Line two baking trays with baking paper.

Place the yams on one of the prepared trays and spread out evenly. Lightly drizzle with olive oil, if using, and season to taste. Bake for 45 minutes, or until yams are golden and tender.

For the Caramelised pecans, place all the ingredients in a small bowl and toss until the pecans are evenly coated. Place on the remaining prepared tray and drizzle over any remaining mixture from the bowl. Spread out evenly and bake for about 8–10 minutes. Watch closely for the last few minutes as they will burn quickly. Remove from the oven and let cool.

To make the salad, sprinkle a handful of rocket leaves on a serving plate, followed by microgreens, red onion, yams, pecans and a drizzle of the Sweet Mustard and Lemon Tahini Dressing. Repeat this process a few more times to build layers with the remaining ingredients. Serve with any remaining dressing on the side.

SUMAC PUMPKIN, CARAMELISED ONIONS AND GREENS WITH ROAST GARLIC DRESSING

SERVES 4–6

Humble ingredients, including wintery warm pumpkin, garden greens, fresh herbs and garlic, come together to create something truly spectacular in this salad. Overloaded with layers upon layers of pure deliciousness, this generous and dreamy salad works perfectly for any occasion. Scrumptious!

Preheat the oven to 180°C (350°F) fan-bake. Line a large baking tray with baking paper.

Place the pumpkin, sumac, cumin and fennel seeds in a large bowl. Lightly drizzle with olive oil, if using, and season to taste. Place on the prepared tray, along with any remaining spice mix, and spread out evenly. Bake for about 45 minutes, or until golden. Leave the oven on to toast the cashews.

While the pumpkin cooks, make the Caramelised onions. Heat the oil, if using, in a large frying pan over medium–high heat. Add the onion and cook for 10 minutes, stirring frequently, until very soft and beginning to caramelise. Add the vinegar and coconut sugar, then reduce heat and continue to cook for 5 minutes, or until the onion is dark brown and caramelised.

Place the cashews on a baking tray and spread out evenly. Bake for about 5–7 minutes, or until golden. Watch closely for the last few minutes as they will burn quickly.

To serve, sprinkle a generous handful of spinach, kale and parsley on a large serving plate, followed by some zucchini ribbons, roast pumpkin, caramelised onions, edamame beans, cashews, hempseeds and a drizzle of the Roast Garlic Dressing. Repeat this process a few more times to build layers with the remaining ingredients. Serve with any remaining dressing on the side.

Tip: *If the Roast Garlic Dressing (page 256) is not prepared before you roast the pumpkin, add the 2 heads of garlic for that dressing to the tray of pumpkin.*

800–900 g (1 lb 12 oz–2 lb) pumpkin (butternut squash, etc.), cut into bite-sized cubes (skins on)
1 teaspoon ground sumac
½ teaspoon cumin seeds
½ teaspoon fennel seeds
olive oil (optional)
sea salt and cracked pepper, to taste
½ cup raw cashews
2 handfuls fresh spinach, finely shredded
handful kale, stems removed, leaves roughly chopped
handful fresh parsley, roughly chopped
1 zucchini, peeled into ribbons
½ cup frozen edamame beans, thawed
2 tablespoons hempseeds
1½ cups Roast Garlic Dressing (page 256), see tip

CARAMELISED ONIONS

1 tablespoon olive or avocado oil (optional)
2 large red onions, finely sliced
2 tablespoons balsamic vinegar
1½ tablespoons coconut sugar (or pure maple syrup)

SERVES 4 OR 6–8 AS A SIDE

SMOKY COCONUT BAKON AND CREAMY RAW BROCCOLI SLAW

COCONUT BAKON

- 1½ cups coconut flakes (coconut chips)
- 2 tablespoons tamari
- 1½ tablespoons pure maple syrup
- 1 tablespoon smoked paprika
- 2 teaspoons apple cider vinegar
- 1 teaspoon garlic powder
- 1 teaspoon onion powder

SUNFLOWER CREAM DRESSING

- 1 cup sunflower seeds, presoaked (see Recipe Notes page 42)
- ½ cup rice milk (or other plant milk)
- 1 large clove garlic
- 3 tablespoons lemon juice
- 2 tablespoons wholegrain mustard
- 1 tablespoon pure maple syrup

SALAD

- 2 heads broccoli, cut into florets, then finely sliced
- ½ small red onion, finely sliced
- 1 spring onion, finely sliced, plus extra to serve
- ⅔ cup dried cranberries
- ¼ cup chopped almonds
- 1 large avocado, stoned and diced

This nourishing vegan take on a classic broccoli and bacon salad comes together quickly and makes a delicious light meal or a unique side. I love the wholesome crunch of raw broccoli in a slaw, especially here, where it's drenched in a creamy sunflower dressing, with chewy cranberries and a generous scattering of the flavourful, crispy coconut. With their smoky barbecue flavour, these crunchy beauties are a little addictive. They make a great snack and an easy flavour bomb that complements any plant-based dish.

Preheat the oven to 180°C (350°F) fan-bake. Line a large baking tray with baking paper.

For the Coconut bakon, place all the ingredients in a bowl and toss to evenly combine. Transfer the mixture to the prepared tray and spread out evenly. Bake, tossing once or twice during cooking, for about 12–13 minutes, or until crispy. Watch closely for the last few minutes as they will burn easily. Remove from the oven and let cool.

For the Sunflower cream dressing, place all the ingredients in a blender and blend for about 30 seconds, or until smooth and creamy.

To make the salad, place the broccoli, onions, cranberries and almonds in a large bowl. Add the dressing and mix to combine. Add the diced avocado and three-quarters of the Coconut bakon, then gently toss through the salad.

To serve, transfer the salad to a serving plate. Scatter over the extra spring onion and remaining Coconut bakon.

INDIAN RICE, CARROT AND ROAST CASHEW WITH CARDAMOM LIME YOGHURT

SERVES 4 OR 6–8 AS A SIDE

This beautiful Bombay-style mixture is the perfect make-ahead salad for a filling packed lunch or simple, wholesome dinner, served alongside fresh greens and sliced avocado. The Cardamom lime yoghurt is a great match for the subtly spiced rice, sweet raisins and crunchy roast cashews. The result is a gorgeous contrast of flavour-packed goodness. This tasty dressing also pairs well with other spice-laden foods, baked potatoes or Buddha bowls.

Preheat the oven to 180°C (350°F) fan-bake. Line a baking tray with baking paper.

Place the rice, water, maple syrup, curry power, garlic powder, turmeric and sea salt in a saucepan and cover. Bring to a boil and, once boiling, reduce heat and simmer for about 25 minutes, or until the water has absorbed and the rice is soft and fluffy.

Spread the cashews evenly around the prepared baking tray and bake for about 5–7 minutes, or until golden. Watch closely for the last few minutes as the cashews will burn quickly.

For the Cardamom lime yoghurt, place all the ingredients in a bowl and mix to combine.

When the rice is cooked, remove the lid and fluff with a fork. Let cool for about 5 minutes.

To make the salad, put the carrots in a large bowl with the spring onion, sultanas, herbs, lemon juice and cumin seeds. Add the cooled rice, two-thirds of the dressing and 1 cup of the roast cashews. Mix to combine.

To serve, transfer to a serving bowl and scatter over the remaining roast cashews. Serve the remaining dressing on the side.

1 cup brown basmati rice
2 cups water
1 tablespoon pure maple syrup
¾ teaspoon mild yellow curry powder
½ teaspoon garlic powder
¼ teaspoon ground turmeric
½ teaspoon sea salt
1¼ cups raw cashews
2 carrots, julienned
3 spring onions, finely sliced
⅔ cup sultanas
1 cup fresh coriander, roughly chopped
handful fresh parsley, roughly chopped
2 tablespoons lemon juice
1 teaspoon cumin seeds

CARDAMOM LIME YOGHURT
1 cup coconut yoghurt
2 tablespoons lime juice
1 teaspoon garlic powder
1 teaspoon onion powder
1 tablespoon tamari
2½ teaspoons pure maple syrup
¼ teaspoon ground cardamom
¼ teaspoon ground ginger

SERVES 4 OR 6–8 AS A SIDE

CINNAMON-SPICED KŪMARA, QUINOA AND ROCKET WITH HEMP MISO AIOLI

2 large orange kūmara (about 900 g/2 lb), cut lengthways into 1–2 cm (½–¾ in) batons
2 teaspoons sesame oil
½ teaspoon ground cinnamon
½ teaspoon ground mixed spice
½ teaspoon dried thyme
½ teaspoon sea salt, plus extra to taste
¾ cup black quinoa
1½ cups water
1 tablespoon lemon juice
2 teaspoons balsamic vinegar
cracked pepper, to taste
3 large handfuls baby rocket leaves
handful fresh mint leaves, finely chopped, plus extra leaves to serve
handful fresh dill, finely chopped
2 spring onions, finely sliced
¼ cup pistachios
1 cup Hemp Miso Aioli (page 252)

If you're looking for an effortlessly thrown together crowd-pleaser that not only packs a punch in both flavour and nutrition but also happens to be aesthetically pleasing on a plate, I've got you covered. The kūmara wedges (which also work well as a delish snack or light bite) are spiced perfectly and make for a delicious duo when teamed up with the creamy Hemp Miso Aioli – a beautiful versatile dressing that sits well with everything. I tend to choose quinoa, which is an earthy gluten-free wholegrain that boasts fibre, protein, iron and magnesium, as a wholesome filler for my salads or bowls, but you can easily leave it out if you're in the mood for a lighter option.

Preheat the oven to 180°C (350°F) fan-bake. Line a large baking tray with baking paper.

Place the kūmara, sesame oil, cinnamon, mixed spice, thyme and salt in a large bowl and toss until the kūmara is well coated in the flavours. Tip onto the prepared tray and spread out in a single layer. Bake for 40–45 minutes, or until golden.

Place the quinoa and water in a saucepan, cover, and bring to a boil. Once boiling, reduce heat to low and simmer for about 12–15 minutes, or until the water has absorbed and the quinoa is soft and fluffy.

Once the quinoa is cooked, add the lemon juice and vinegar to the saucepan, and season to taste.

To serve, sprinkle a generous handful of rocket, herbs and spring onion on a large serving plate, followed by some of the quinoa and kūmara, a sprinkle of pistachios and a drizzle of the Hemp Miso Aioli. Repeat this process a few more times to build layers with the remaining ingredients, then top with extra mint leaves. Serve with any extra dressing on the side.

SERVES 4–6

CREAMY KALE AND POTATO WEDGES WITH CRANBERRIES, CAPERS AND DILL RANCH

6 large agria potatoes, cut into wedges
olive oil (optional)
sea salt and cracked pepper, to taste
3 cups roughly chopped curly kale leaves or cavolo nero
3 stalks celery, sliced
1 red onion, finely sliced
2 spring onions, finely sliced
handful fresh dill, finely chopped, plus extra to serve
handful fresh parsley, finely chopped, plus extra to serve
3 tablespoons capers, drained
½ cup dried cranberries (or raisins)
1 teaspoon sea salt
1 cup Creamy Dill Ranch Dressing (page 252) or Hemp Miso Aioli (page 252)

I have a real soft spot for creamy kale salads and also for creamy potato salads (who doesn't?), so I decided to combine the two and create this winning combo. If there was ever a salad for the whole family to enjoy, this would have to be the one. It ticks all the boxes with its perfect balance of comforting potato wedges, refreshing herbs and kale, salty capers and chewy cranberries for that extra bite of sweetness, all generously dressed in an indulgent, Creamy Dill Ranch Dressing (page 252). It's a flavourful favourite that is sure to become a reliable staple in your home.

Preheat the oven to 180°C (350°F). Line a large baking tray with baking paper.

Place the potato wedges onto the prepared tray and spread out evenly. Lightly drizzle with olive oil, if using, and season to taste. Bake for 40 minutes, or until golden.

To make the salad, place the potatoes, kale, celery, onions, herbs, capers, cranberries and salt in a large bowl. Add the dressing and season with cracked pepper. Gently toss to combine.

To serve, transfer to a serving plate and lightly sprinkle with extra herbs, and another light season of cracked pepper.

SIMPLE, WHOLESOME QUINOA SALAD

SERVES 4 OR 6–8 AS A SIDE

So simple but oh, so good! Here's a true example of how a basic selection of humble wholefoods can come together to create easy deliciousness. My go-to salad for a quick family dinner also showcases how an alkalising lemon can be the star when dressing a salad. It originally came to life during a family trip through Europe when I found it to be a fabulous travel salad. Wherever we were in the world, we were almost always guaranteed to find the ingredients. With minimal effort, this staple salad makes for an easy, weekday lunch or an on-the-go healthy bite.

Place the quinoa and water in a saucepan, cover, and bring to a boil. Once boiling, reduce heat to low and simmer for about 12–15 minutes, or until the water has absorbed and the quinoa is soft and fluffy.

To make the salad, place all the ingredients in a serving bowl with the cooked quinoa and toss to combine. Adjust the seasonings, if desired.

¾ cup tri-coloured quinoa
1½ cups water
½ large telegraph cucumber, finely diced
2 large tomatoes, finely diced
½ small red onion, finely diced
2 large avocados, stoned and diced
3 handfuls baby spinach leaves, finely chopped
3 tablespoons lemon juice
¾–1 teaspoon sea salt
cracked pepper, to taste

SERVES 4 OR 6–8 AS A SIDE

SUPERGREENS CHUNKY GUACAMOLE SALAD

½ small red onion, roughly chopped
2 cloves garlic
2 cups roughly chopped curly kale leaves or cavolo nero
250 g (9 oz) baby spinach leaves
large handful fresh basil leaves
1½ cups finely diced tomatoes
2–3 large avocados, stoned and finely diced
½ small telegraph cucumber, finely diced
1 large spring onion, finely sliced
¼ cup lemon juice
1 teaspoon sea salt
⅛ teaspoon ground white pepper
cracked pepper, to taste

Allow me to introduce you to my insanely popular, green-boasting signature salad! I absolutely adore the freshness and hydration bouncing around inside this powerhouse of nutrition. The avocado works as a creamy binder while the basil, lemon juice and sea salt are all that's needed to bring the plate to life. It makes eating an abundance of alkalising greens in one sitting incredibly easy and delicious. Ideally, you want to cut the greens ultra-finely using a food processor, which will also allow this salad to come together very quickly, but don't worry if you don't have one; chopping the produce by hand will also work. My son Eli and I have loved this salad for years now!

Place the red onion and garlic in a food processor, then pack in the kale, spinach and basil. Pulse for about 10–15 seconds. Watch carefully for the last few seconds as the spinach will liquify quickly. The greens should resemble a super-fine tabouli-like salad, but if blended for too long, they can turn to mush.

Transfer to a serving bowl along with all other ingredients and toss to combine. Serve immediately.

Tip: *This salad is best served immediately. If making it in advance, simply add the salt and lemon juice just prior to serving as these ingredients will naturally draw out the liquid from the greens.*

SERVES 4 OR 6–8 AS A SIDE

WALDORF CHICKPEA AND POPPYSEED SLAW

1 cup Creamy Dill Ranch Dressing (page 252)

POPPYSEED SLAW

2 x 400 g (14 oz) cans chickpeas, drained and rinsed (or 3 cups cooked chickpeas)
2 cups shredded red cabbage
1 cup finely sliced celery
1 large green apple, cored and diced
½ red onion, finely diced
handful fresh parsley, finely chopped
½ cup sultanas (or raisins)
⅓ cup crushed walnuts
2 tablespoons poppyseeds
sea salt and cracked pepper, to taste

As you probably know, a Waldorf salad is a fruit and nut salad generously dressed in mayonnaise. Traditionally, it's served as an appetiser or a light meal. Here's my modified plant-based alternative, tweaked into a slaw with my cashew-based Creamy Dil Ranch Dressing (page 252). The addition of chickpeas as a protein component makes it bulky enough to serve as a light main. I like to use red cabbage in this tasty slaw, but you can also replace it with green cabbage to harmonise the colour palette of the dish.

Make the dressing first then set aside while you make the slaw.

Place all the slaw ingredients in a large bowl. Pour over the dressing and mix until all ingredients are thoroughly combined in the dressing. Season to taste.

To serve, transfer to a serving bowl and enjoy.

SERVES 6–8 AS A SIDE

BEAUTIFUL RAW MARINATED MUSHROOM CEVICHE

400 g (14 oz) button mushrooms, finely sliced
½ small red onion, finely sliced
1½ cups finely chopped parsley
1 tablespoon fresh thyme leaves

MARINADE
¼ cup olive oil
5 tablespoons apple cider vinegar
3 tablespoons pure maple syrup
2 tablespoons wholegrain mustard
sea salt and cracked pepper, to taste

TO SERVE
½ cup cooked quinoa (optional)
sliced avocado

This gorgeous recipe was originally given to me by my dear friend Nicole. She grew up in a home surrounded by wild field mushrooms so she and her family would often create exotic mushroom recipes. This flavoursome salad is an awesome way to include the benefits of raw mushrooms into your diet. Texturally different to cooked mushrooms, the mildly marinated mushrooms in this salad boast the flavours of their punchy, sweet and tangy dressing. The result is a delightfully wholesome salad that is amazing served with or without the hearty quinoa. Either way, I like to eat this delicious salad topped with creamy avocado.

Put the mushrooms, onion, parsley and fresh thyme leaves in a large bowl and toss to combine.

For the marinade, whisk all the ingredients together in a small bowl and season to taste.

Pour the marinade over the salad and mix well to combine. Cover and place in the fridge to marinate for at least 30–60 minutes.

To serve, remove the salad from the fridge and drain any excess liquid. Mix again. If serving with quinoa, toss through. Top with sliced avocado and enjoy.

REPLENISHING BEETROOT QUINOA

SERVES 4 OR 6–8 AS A SIDE

Requiring minimal ingredients and only 15 minutes prep time, this speedy salad is a harmonious balance of texture, taste, colour and nutrition. I recommend making it for a quick replenisher when you feel in need of a health boost. Raw beetroot is both hydrating and refreshing, and boasts a stellar list of beneficial properties. When combined with the soft quinoa, it creates a nutrient-dense salad that encompasses simple, natural flavours.

Place the quinoa and water in a saucepan, cover, and bring to a boil. Once boiling, reduce heat to low and simmer for about 12–15 minutes, or until the water has absorbed and the quinoa is soft and fluffy.

To make the salad, place all the ingredients in a serving bowl and gently toss to combine. Taste and adjust the seasonings if desired. Serve with a scatter of fresh dill.

1 cup red quinoa
2 cups water
1 large beetroot (about 350 g/12 oz), peeled and grated
1 teaspoon ground cumin
3 tablespoons lime or lemon juice
1 tablespoon balsamic vinegar
2 teaspoons pure maple syrup
handful fresh dill, finely chopped, plus extra to serve
1 teaspoon sea salt
½ teaspoon dried thyme
cracked pepper, to taste

SERVES 4 OR 6–8 AS A SIDE

BROWN RICE SESAME SUSHI SALAD

1 cup brown rice
2 cups water
¼ cup sliced almonds
3 tablespoons black sesame seeds
¼ cup rice vinegar (or brown rice vinegar or rice wine vinegar)
3 tablespoons coconut sugar
¼ teaspoon sea salt
¾ teaspoon finely grated fresh ginger
1 small red capsicum, finely diced
2 spring onions, finely sliced
1 carrot, julienned, then finely chopped
½ small telegraph cucumber, finely diced

TO SERVE
sliced avocado

Milo, my beautiful boy and very fussy eater, particularly enjoys this light bite as it's a true relative of sushi in the form of a wholesome salad. Sushi is traditionally composed of white rice, but I encourage you to try it with brown rice; an unprocessed wholegrain boasting nutrients such as fibre, magnesium and protein. With only a handful of fresh and flavourful, sushi-inspired ingredients, this quick and easy throw-together dish can be enjoyed as an entrée, side dish or as a light meal topped with lots of sliced avocado.

Put the rice and water in a saucepan, cover, and bring to a boil. Once boiling, reduce the heat to low and simmer for about 25 minutes, or until the water is absorbed and the rice is soft.

Meanwhile, heat a frying pan over medium heat. Add the almonds and sesame seeds and cook, tossing frequently to avoid burning, for about 2 minutes, or until toasted and fragrant. Set aside.

Once the rice is cooked, add the vinegar, sugar and salt and gently mix through the rice. Leave to cool slightly.

To make the salad, add the rest of the ingredients, reserving some sesame seeds to garnish, and toss to combine.

To serve, transfer to a serving bowl and top with sliced avocado and reserved sesame seeds.

**SERVES 2–3
GENEROUSLY OR
4 AS A SIDE**

CASHEW AND SUN-DRIED TOMATO PESTO PASTA WITH FRESH BASIL AND AVOCADO

250 g (9 oz) gluten-free penne (I use brown rice or quinoa pasta)
1 cup Chunky Cashew and Sun-dried Tomato Pesto (page 242)
handful fresh basil leaves
¼ cup pitted black or green olives, sliced

TO SERVE
1 large avocado, stoned and sliced
cracked pepper

Here is a classic penne pasta lunch box salad with a delicious (and quite addictive) twist: my Chunky Cashew and Sun-dried Tomato Pesto (page 242). My older boys enjoy this salad for an easy weekday dinner, and if you already have the pesto prepared, it comes together quite quickly and barely makes a dent in the kitchen sink. You can easily double this recipe to create a larger potluck dish or salad for a barbecue. We love this served with lots of fresh, aromatic basil, creamy avocado and cracked pepper.

Bring a large saucepan of water to a boil. Add the pasta and cook according to the packet instructions (about 10–15 minutes). Drain, then rinse under cold water and drain again.

Put the pasta and pesto in a large bowl and gently mix until pasta is evenly coated. Add the basil leaves and olives and toss through.

To serve, transfer to a shallow serving bowl and top with sliced avocado and cracked pepper.

EVERYDAY MAINS

EVERYDAY MAINS

The following pages radiate simple, soul-hugging lunch and dinner ideas packed with plant-based nutrition and deliciousness for easy everyday meals. Practicality was at the forefront when designing the recipes in this chapter, and they're curated in a variety of popular, modern cuisines to suit all ages and diets, whether omnivore, vegetarian or vegan. Basic vegetables, herbs and spices take centre stage, combined with many of the staples from The Wholefoods Kitchen (page 22). Don't be afraid to tweak a recipe with what you have on hand; they're all really versatile. You can easily substitute any of the vegetables or fresh herbs with in-season produce locally grown in your area.

    The recipes in this chapter are designed to feed at least four people, and although most can be halved for a smaller serving, I do encourage you to make the full recipe as any leftovers can be refrigerated (or even frozen) for a wholesome, ready-to-go lunch or dinner over the following days. I hope you enjoy the heart-warming, plant-based goodness throughout this chapter, and that the recipes become rewarding everyday favourites in your home.

Traybakes

I encourage you to experiment in the kitchen with plant-based traybakes – a simple tray of baked wholefoods in a wide variety of flavours and textures. What I love about them is that they create a quick, fuss-free and cost-effective meal with extremely minimal preparation (often less than 10 minutes) and very little kitchen clean-up. Simply throw everything on a large dish, and bake! They're a nutritious, handy tool for those busy weekday evenings and an effective way to increase your veggie intake. A traybake is also a simple way to build a substantial salad base. I like to serve mine with extra raw goodness tossed through in the form of microgreens, sprouts, avocado and of course, an array of delicious homemade dressings. With veggies being the hero ingredient, there are endless variations to explore using a selection of your favourite wholefoods. I have included a few easy recipes throughout this chapter, but let's break down the basics of conquering your very own crowd-pleasing trays that will hopefully become reliable weekly staples.

My go-to, nutritious traybake method for a quick, easy and delicious meal

1. Choose an array of fresh vegetables. I usually choose anywhere between two and six veggies. Feel free to add more, but keep in mind that even the simplest of trays can create a big impact. This is also a great opportunity to experiment with seasonal veggies, or to use up any produce that needs eating.

2. Choose an optional legume such as chickpeas, lentils or black beans. Or, for a creative and refreshing bite, try adding jackfruit.

3. Select a handful of nutritional seeds to scatter over the veggies before (or after) baking. My favourites include sesame seeds, pumpkin seeds and sunflower seeds.

4. Add some optional extras, including flavour boosters such as olives or capers for a salty element, dates or cranberries for that bite of chewy sweetness, or seasonings such as dried herbs, spices, salt and pepper.

5. Select a dressing. Have a flick through the Super Salads chapter (page 70) and/or the Dips and Dressings chapter (page 232) and select a delicious dressing. Although this is an optional step, there are some epic, hassle-free recipes throughout this book to satisfy your palate and take your traybake to another level.

6. Put it all together. This is the fun part! Simply spread everything out on a large baking tray and bake until tender. Serve with a scatter of any of the following: fresh baby spinach or rocket leaves, sprouts, microgreens, fresh herbs, chopped nuts or sliced avocado, and then finish with a generous drizzle of your selected dressing. Traybakes can also be served with a gluten-free wholegrain tossed through, such as millet, quinoa or buckwheat – it's the perfect way to create a hassle-free, hearty salad. Store any leftovers in a sealed container in the fridge for up to five days.

CHUNKY LENTIL DAHL WITH SWEET APRICOT, ROAST CAULIFLOWER AND FRESH MINT

SERVES 4

1 head cauliflower, cut into small florets
olive or avocado oil (optional)
2 teaspoons black mustard seeds
1 brown onion, diced
4 cloves garlic, finely chopped
3 cm (1¼ in) piece fresh ginger, peeled and finely chopped
2 teaspoons ground cumin
2 teaspoons curry powder
1 teaspoon ground cinnamon
½ teaspoon ground cardamom
¼ teaspoon ground cloves
1 teaspoon paprika
1 teaspoon sea salt
¼ teaspoon cracked pepper
1 cup dried red lentils, rinsed
3 cups water
2 tablespoons pure maple syrup
400 ml (14 fl oz) can coconut milk
⅔ cup chopped dried apricots
2 tablespoons lime juice
2 cups baby spinach leaves
handful fresh mint leaves, plus extra to serve

TO SERVE (OPTIONAL)
lime zest
chilli flakes
garden greens (spinach, kale, rocket, etc.)
diced avocado
brown rice

Indian spices, creamy coconut milk, roast cauliflower, lentils and sweet apricots create a beautiful bowlful of delish flavours and textures that will warm you from the inside out. The apricots really do add a gorgeous, sweet touch that I find work wonders in this chunky, palate-pleasing dahl. It can be served simply, with fresh mint and diced avocado or fresh greens, but is equally as good served over brown rice for a heartier lunch or dinner. Enjoy any leftovers the following day as the flavours will continue to mingle and strengthen with time. This beautiful dahl also freezes well.

Preheat the oven to 180°C (350°F) fan-bake. Line a large baking tray with baking paper.

Place the cauliflower on the baking tray and spread out in a single layer. Lightly drizzle with oil, if using, and season to taste. Bake for 20–25 minutes, or until tender.

Heat the oil, if using, in a large frying pan over medium–high heat. Add the mustard seeds and cook for 1–2 minutes, until the seeds become fragrant and begin to pop. Add the onion, garlic and ginger and cook for 5–7 minutes, stirring frequently, until soft and fragrant. Add the spices, salt and pepper, mix through and cook for a further 2 minutes.

Add the lentils, water and maple syrup and stir to combine. Reduce the heat to low and simmer, stirring frequently, for about 25 minutes or until the lentils are soft.

Add the cauliflower, coconut milk and most of the apricots and continue to simmer on low heat for a further 10–12 minutes, until the dahl has thickened slightly. Finally, stir through the lime juice, spinach leaves and fresh mint leaves.

To serve, top with lime zest and chilli flakes and serve with a side of avocado, garden greens or brown rice, if using. Garnish with the reserved apricot and extra mint leaves.

SERVES 4

POST-SURF JACKFRUIT AND KŪMARA RED THAI CURRY

1 large purple kūmara, cut into bite-sized cubes
1 teaspoon olive or avocado oil (optional)
1 brown onion, diced
3 cloves garlic, chopped
1 tablespoon finely chopped fresh ginger
1 large red capsicum, sliced lengthways into strips
400 g (14 oz) can young jackfruit, drained
1–2 tablespoons coconut sugar (optional)
1 head broccoli, cut into small florets

THAI RED CURRY SAUCE
4 spring onions, trimmed
1 red capsicum, deseeded
2 makrut lime leaves
2 cloves garlic, peeled
3 cm (1¼ in) piece fresh ginger, peeled
1 teaspoon ground turmeric
1 teaspoon ground coriander
1 teaspoon ground cumin
½ teaspoon cracked pepper
¼ cup tamari
3 tablespoons pure maple syrup
3 tablespoons peanut butter
400 ml (14 fl oz) can coconut milk

I live in a home of keen surfers who often come in from our very chilly New Zealand waters ready for something hearty and warming, especially in the cooler months. For Ricardo, who loves a good plant-based hot pot, a comforting curry always hits the spot. This sweet and flavoursome mingle comes together with ease and is surprisingly quick to make from scratch. The kūmara and jackfruit are the essential duo in this recipe, and when combined with the luscious creamy Thai sauce, they create a mild, homely curry everyone will enjoy. This would have to be up there as a strong contender for my favourite in this chapter.

Bring a saucepan half-filled with water to a boil. Place the kūmara in a colander over the water, cover, and steam for 15 minutes, or until just tender.

For the Thai red curry sauce, place all the ingredients in a blender and blend for about 20–30 seconds, or until smooth. Set aside.

Heat the oil, if using, in a large frying pan over medium–high heat. Add the onion, garlic and ginger, and cook for 5–7 minutes, stirring frequently, until the mixture is soft and fragrant. Add the capsicum and continue to cook for a further 1–2 minutes. Gently stir through the jackfruit and kūmara.

Stir in the Thai red curry sauce, along with the coconut sugar, if using. (I like to add coconut sugar for a touch of extra sweetness.) Simmer, stirring occasionally, for about 5 minutes. Add the broccoli and continue to simmer for a further 5–7 minutes, or until the sauce has thickened and the veggies are just tender.

Serve over a bed of garden greens or brown rice and garnish with fresh coriander, if desired.

SERVES 4

ALMOND MISO-GLAZED EGGPLANT BOATS WITH LIME AND BASIL RICE SALAD

4 eggplants, halved lengthways, then scored diagonally

ALMOND MISO GLAZE

¼ cup white miso paste
2 tablespoons tamari
2 tablespoons pure maple syrup
2 tablespoons almond butter
1 teaspoon finely grated fresh ginger
1 tablespoon apple cider vinegar
1 tablespoon sesame oil
1 teaspoon garlic granules
2 tablespoons hot water

LIME AND BASIL RICE SALAD

1 cup black rice
2 cups water
1 red capsicum, finely diced
1 cup fresh basil leaves, finely chopped
½ cup fresh coriander leaves, finely chopped
2 spring onions, finely sliced
3 tablespoons lime juice
1 tablespoon lime zest
2 tablespoons sesame seeds
½ teaspoon sea salt
¼–½ teaspoon chilli flakes (optional), plus extra to serve

TO SERVE

diced avocado
coconut yoghurt

I adore this Japanese-inspired dish. Whether you're a fan of eggplant or not, I suspect you'll fall in love with these sweet and salty, and slightly charred caramelised boats. They're coated in a creamy miso glaze then topped with an antioxidant-rich salad for a crisp and refreshing contrast. Beautiful black rice delivers a wonderful freshness thanks to the large quantities of basil and lime, and it perfectly balances out the bold and punchy flavours of the baked eggplant to create an easy and substantially wholesome lunch or dinner.

Preheat the oven to 180°C (350°F) fan-bake.

For the Almond miso glaze, mix all ingredients in a bowl until smooth and creamy.

Place the eggplants, flesh-side up, into a large glass baking dish and evenly pour over two-thirds of the glaze. Set the rest aside for dressing the salad later. Cover the baking dish with foil and bake for 45–50 minutes, or until the eggplant is tender and the marinade is beginning to caramelise.

For the Lime and basil rice salad, place the rice and water in a medium saucepan, cover, and bring to a boil. Reduce heat and simmer for about 25 minutes, or until the water has absorbed and the rice is soft. Remove the lid, and let cool for 5–10 minutes.

Add the other salad ingredients to the saucepan, along with the remaining glaze. Toss to combine.

To serve, place two eggplant halves on each plate and top with a few generous spoonfuls of the rice salad. Finish with diced avocado, a dollop of coconut yoghurt and a sprinkle of chilli flakes, if using.

BOMBAY JACKFRUIT AND CRISPY POTATO MINGLE WITH APPLE, LIME AND CORIANDER CHUTNEY

SERVES 4–6

This epic play on Bombay potatoes is quite an extraordinary throw-together meal that can be served hot, straight out of the oven, or cold for a large salad. It encompasses four distinct flavours: sweet, sour, salt and spicy, which, along with numerous textures, morph into a glorious dish for lunch or dinner. The chutney is incredibly refreshing and can either be tossed through the potatoes and jackfruit or served on the side. (I usually toss half of it through and serve the remainder on the side.)

Preheat the oven to 180°C (350°F) fan-bake. Line a large baking tray with baking paper.

Bring a saucepan half-filled with water to a boil. Place the potatoes in a colander over the water, cover, and steam for 15 minutes, or until just tender. Transfer to the prepared tray. Lightly drizzle with oil, if using, and season to taste. Bake for 25–30 minutes, or until golden and crispy.

For the chutney, place all the ingredients in a food processor and blend for about 25–30 seconds, or until it becomes a chunky chutney. You may need to stop the food processor, scrape down the sides, then blend again. Set aside.

When the potatoes are about 10 minutes away from being ready, heat a tablespoon of oil, if using, in a large frying pan over medium–high heat. Add the onion and cumin seeds and cook for about 5–7 minutes, stirring frequently, until the onion is soft and fragrant. Add the jackfruit, curry powder, maple syrup, salt and turmeric. Toss to combine and continue to cook for 2 minutes. Add the spinach and cook for a further 1–2 minutes, or until the spinach is just wilted.

Put the potatoes in a large bowl with the jackfruit mixture, coconut yoghurt and half the Apple, lime and coriander chutney, and toss to combine.

To serve, transfer to a serving plate. Sprinkle over the sliced spring onion. Finish with a dollop of coconut yoghurt and serve the remaining chutney on the side.

700–800 g (1 lb 9 oz–1 lb 12 oz) baby potatoes, halved (or agria potatoes cut into small cubes)
olive or avocado oil (optional)
sea salt and cracked pepper, to taste
1 large red onion, finely sliced
½ teaspoon cumin seeds
2 x 400 g (14 oz) cans young jackfruit, drained and broken into smaller pieces
1 tablespoon mild yellow curry powder
2½ tablespoons pure maple syrup
½ teaspoon sea salt
¼ teaspoon ground turmeric
120 g (4½ oz) spinach leaves, roughly chopped
¼ cup coconut yoghurt, plus extra to serve
1 spring onion, finely sliced, to serve

APPLE, LIME AND CORIANDER CHUTNEY

2 cups fresh coriander
1 large granny smith apple
½ small green chilli (optional)
2 cloves garlic
1 tablespoon chopped fresh ginger
2 tablespoons lime juice
½ teaspoon sea salt

TASTY QUINOA AND LENTIL BALLS WITH EASY MARINARA SAUCE

SERVES 4

QUINOA AND LENTIL BALLS
½ cup red quinoa
1 cup water
olive or avocado oil (optional)
1 large brown onion, finely diced
3 cloves garlic, finely chopped
400 g (14 oz) can brown lentils, drained and rinsed (or 1½ cups cooked lentils)
2 carrots, finely grated, excess liquid squeezed out
3 tablespoons buckwheat flour or chickpea flour (besan)
3 tablespoons nutritional yeast
2 tablespoons tomato paste
2 tablespoons tamari
1 tablespoon paprika
1 tablespoon sumac
2 teaspoons dried oregano
½–1 teaspoon sea salt

MARINARA SAUCE
2 x 400 g (14 oz) cans chopped tomatoes
1 cup water
small handful fresh basil leaves, plus extra to serve
2 large cloves garlic
3 tablespoons nutritional yeast
2 tablespoons pure maple syrup
1 teaspoon dried oregano
½ teaspoon sea salt
½ teaspoon onion powder

TO SERVE (OPTIONAL)
gluten-free pasta or brown rice
Cheesy Rosemary Crumble (page 152)

These flavourful, plant-based balls are nutrient-dense and protein-packed thanks to lentils and quinoa. Easily put together, they're a versatile number that make for a scrumptious, earthy bite the whole family can enjoy. They are wonderful immersed in the quick and easy marinara sauce here, with a side of fresh rocket leaves and gluten-free noodles or brown rice. They can also be served in a gluten-free wrap with my creamy Hemp Miso Aioli (page 252) or Avocado Mayo (page 249), or simply paired with the beautiful Coriander Cream on page 246 for a snack or lunch-box filler.

Place the quinoa and water in a saucepan, cover, and bring to a boil. Once boiling, reduce the heat to low and simmer for 12–15 minutes, or until the water has absorbed and the quinoa is soft and fluffy.

Heat a teaspoon of oil, if using, in a large frying pan over medium–high heat. Add the onion and garlic and cook for 5–7 minutes, stirring frequently, until soft and fragrant. Transfer to a large bowl along with all other Quinoa and lentil ball ingredients and mix to combine well.

Preheat the oven to 180°C (350°F) fan-bake. Line a large baking tray with baking paper.

Using your hands, roll the mixture into 20 balls (slightly smaller than a golf ball). Place on the prepared tray and bake for about 30 minutes, or until they are beginning to crisp around the sides.

For the Marinara sauce, place all the ingredients in a blender and blend for about 20 seconds, or until smooth. Heat a large saucepan over medium–high heat. Add the sauce and bring to a boil. Reduce heat and simmer, stirring occasionally, for 25–30 minutes, until thickened.

Serve the balls on a bed of gluten-free spaghetti or brown rice. Drizzle over the Marinara sauce and finish with extra basil leaves and a sprinkle of the Cheesy Rosemary Crumble, if using.

CREAMY ALFREDO SPAGHETTI WITH CARAMELISED ONION, BROCCOLI AND CHEESY KALE

SERVES 4

1 head broccoli, cut into florets
250 g (9 oz) gluten-free spaghetti

CHEESY KALE

1 bunch curly kale or cavolo nero, stems removed, leaves roughly chopped
2 teaspoons olive oil
2 tablespoons nutritional yeast
sea salt and cracked pepper, to taste
¼ cup fresh thyme leaves
¼–½ teaspoon chilli flakes (optional)

CARAMELISED ONIONS

1 tablespoon olive or avocado oil (optional)
2 large red onions, sliced
2 tablespoons balsamic vinegar
1½ tablespoons coconut sugar or pure maple syrup

CREAMY ALFREDO SAUCE

1 cup raw cashews, presoaked (see Recipe Notes page 42)
¾ cup rice milk (or other plant milk)
½ cup nutritional yeast
2 stalks celery
2 tablespoons lemon juice
2 cloves garlic
1 tablespoon wholegrain mustard
1 tablespoon fresh rosemary leaves
¼ teaspoon sea salt

You can definitely count on this comforting pasta for an easy weekday dinner. There are many things to love about it, from the cheesy, crispy kale to the caramelised onion, flavourful alfredo sauce and aromatic fresh thyme; each element does its part to create a heavenly pasta dish everyone will love. For an extra flavour booster, serve with a generous sprinkle of the parmesan-like Cheesy Rosemary Crumble (page 152).

Preheat the oven to 180°C (350°F) fan-bake. Line a large baking tray with baking paper.

For the Cheesy kale, place the kale or cavolo nero and oil in a large bowl. Use your hands to massage the oil into the leaves for about 1 minute, or until they begin to soften. Add the nutritional yeast, season to taste and massage the flavours into the leaves until evenly coated. Set aside.

Place the broccoli on the prepared tray and spread out in a single layer. Bake for 10 minutes. Add the kale to the broccoli and bake for a further 10 minutes, or until the broccoli is just tender, and the kale is wilted and slightly charred. Watch closely for the last few minutes as the kale will burn quickly.

Bring a large saucepan of water to a boil. Add the pasta and cook according to the packet instructions (about 10–15 minutes).

For the Caramelised onion, heat the oil, if using, in a large frying pan over medium–high heat. Add the onion and cook for 10 minutes, stirring frequently, until very soft and starting to caramelise. Add the vinegar and coconut sugar, reduce heat and continue to cook for a further 5 minutes, or until the onion mixture is dark brown and caramelised.

For the Creamy alfredo sauce, place all the ingredients in a blender and blend for 30 seconds, or until smooth and creamy.

Drain the pasta and transfer to a large serving bowl. Add the caramelised onion, broccoli and cheesy kale, fresh thyme leaves and chilli flakes (if using), then pour over the sauce. Gently mix everything together until well combined.

SMOKY SPINACH CREAM CHEESE SMASHED POTATOES

SERVES 4–6

Ricardo dreams of these irresistible creamy potatoes; they're truly moreish and a firm family favourite. With minimal effort, you can rely on this recipe for a quick crowd-pleaser served alongside a fresh garden salad. To serve as an appetiser, simply dollop the dip over smashed baby potatoes to create smaller, bite-sized treats. The Smoky Spinach Cream Cheese (page 238) is divine, with its piquant, lemony kick and a cheesy, smoky flavour. It's also fabulous starred in the centre of a cob loaf, paired with wholefood crackers and veggie sticks or smothered over a wholesome sandwich.

8 medium agria potatoes
olive or avocado oil (optional)
sea salt and cracked pepper, to taste
1½ cups Smoky Spinach Cream Cheese (page 238)

TO SERVE (OPTIONAL)
chilli flakes
finely sliced spring onion or chives
diced red capsicum
garden greens (spinach, kale, rocket, etc.)
sliced avocado

Bring a large saucepan of water to a boil. Add the potatoes and cook for about 20–25 minutes, or until fork tender. Drain.

Preheat the oven to 180°C (350°F) fan-bake. Line a large baking tray with baking paper.

Place the potatoes on the prepared tray and gently smash them down with the base of a saucepan. Lightly drizzle with oil, if using, and season to taste. Place in the oven and bake for 25 minutes, until golden brown and crispy around the edges.

While the potatoes cook, make the Smoky Spinach Cream Cheese if you haven't already prepared it.

To serve, divide the potatoes between serving plates and then spoon some Smoky Spinach Cream Cheese evenly over each potato. Add any of the delicious topping suggestions. Serve with a side of garden greens and sliced avocado, if desired.

SERVES 4–6

BANANA BLOSSOM, LEEK AND KŪMARA CRUSTLESS PIE WITH CHEESY ROSEMARY CRUMBLE

2 purple kūmara (about 650 g/1 lb 7 oz), cut into bite-sized cubes
1 tablespoon olive or avocado oil (optional)
2 large leeks, green ends discarded, whites finely sliced
1 brown onion, finely sliced
2 cloves garlic, finely chopped
200 g (7 oz) fresh spinach, roughly chopped (or use baby spinach leaves)
1 tablespoon fresh rosemary leaves, roughly chopped
1 teaspoon mixed spice
½ teaspoon sea salt
2 x 400 g (14 oz) cans banana blossom, drained, rinsed and roughly chopped

SUNFLOWER CREAM

1 cup sunflower seeds, presoaked (see Recipe Notes page 42)
3 tablespoons lemon juice
1 clove garlic
¼ cup white miso paste
1 cup rice milk (or other plant milk)

CHEESY ROSEMARY CRUMBLE

½ cup raw cashews
¼ cup sesame seeds
2 tablespoons nutritional yeast
1 tablespoon white miso paste
1 teaspoon dried rosemary

'What on earth is banana blossom?' you ask. Don't worry, I assure you it's really easy to stumble upon in most supermarkets. Quite similar to jackfruit, banana blossom is a fleshy, purple-skinned flower, which grows at the end of a banana cluster. Traditionally used in South-east Asian and Indian cooking, it's now widely popular as a vegan substitute for fish, due to its flaky, chunky texture. So here, my friends, is my finger-licking, creamy crustless pie, which also features caramelised leek, fresh rosemary, light spices and chunks of sweet kūmara, all immersed in a rich sunflower, miso sauce and finished with a layer of the parmesan-like Cheesy Rosemary Crumble. The crumble is absolutely divine and also works well sprinkled over pasta, pizzas and salads. Do not put this gloriously cosy winter's pie in the too-hard basket, it truly is very simple to put together and so delicious.

Bring a saucepan half-filled with water to a boil. Place the kūmara in a colander over the water, cover and steam for 15 minutes, or until just tender.

Heat the oil, if using, in a large frying pan over medium–high heat. Add the leek, onion and garlic and cook for about 10 minutes, stirring frequently, until soft and fragrant. Add the spinach, rosemary, mixed spice and salt and continue to cook for a further 1–2 minutes.

For the Sunflower cream, place all the ingredients in a blender and blend for about 30 seconds, or until smooth and creamy.

For the Cheesy rosemary crumble, place all the ingredients in a food processor and blend for about 30 seconds, or until it's a fine parmesan-like crumble.

Preheat the oven to 180°C (350°F) fan-bake.

Transfer the leek mixture to a large bowl along with the banana blossom, kūmara and Sunflower cream. Gently mix to combine. Transfer to a deep pie dish and spread out evenly. Sprinkle over the rosemary crumble. Bake for about 20 minutes, until golden.

SERVES 6

THE ULTIMATE HEARTY AND FLAVOURFUL VEGAN SHEPHERD'S PIE

POTATO TOPPING

6 large potatoes, peeled and cut into cubes
1 cup rice milk (or other plant milk)
½ teaspoon sea salt
⅛ teaspoon ground white pepper

SHEPHERD'S PIE FILLING

1 tablespoon olive or avocado oil (optional)
1 tablespoon coriander seeds
1 brown onion, diced
3 cloves garlic, finely chopped
2 cups sliced mushrooms
1 cup sliced celery
1 zucchini, grated
2 large carrots, grated
1 tablespoon fresh rosemary leaves, finely chopped
1 tablespoon fresh thyme leaves
1 teaspoon ground cumin
2 x 400 g (14 oz) cans brown lentils, drained and rinsed (or 3 cups cooked lentils)
⅓ cup tomato paste
2 tablespoons tamari
2 tablespoons nutritional yeast
2 tablespoons balsamic vinegar
1 tablespoon Dijon mustard
⅔ cup rice milk (or other plant milk)
1½ tablespoons buckwheat flour (or other gluten-free flour)
sea salt and cracked pepper

My scrumptious, veganised take on the traditional shepherd's pie is another one of those heartwarming dishes I like to make in the cooler months – one that will have you coming back to it for comfort and sustenance. Although the ingredients list is lengthy, it's really just a simple collection of wintery vegetables and hearty lentils combined with a handful of common pantry staples. The added touch of fresh rosemary and thyme imparts a wonderful herby essence. I like to serve this hearty family meal with a side of fresh garden greens and sliced avocado, as always.

For the Potato topping, bring a saucepan half-filled with water to a boil. Place the potato in a colander over the water, cover, and steam for 20 minutes, or until tender.

For the Shepherd's pie filling, heat the oil, if using, in a large frying pan over medium–high heat. Add the coriander seeds and cook for 1–2 minutes, or until the seeds become fragrant and begin to pop. Add the onion and garlic and cook for 5–7 minutes, stirring frequently, until soft and fragrant. Add the mushrooms and continue to cook for another 2 minutes. Add the celery, zucchini, carrot, rosemary, thyme and cumin, and cook for a further 6–8 minutes, or until the celery, zucchini and carrot are tender.

Reduce the heat to low and add the lentils, tomato paste, tamari, nutritional yeast, vinegar, mustard, rice milk and flour then season to taste. Mix until everything is well combined.

Transfer to a deep pie dish and spread out evenly.

Preheat the oven to 180°C (350°F) fan-bake.

Drain the potato. Transfer to a large bowl with the rice milk, salt and pepper, and mash until smooth and creamy. Spread evenly over the lentil mixture. Bake for 25–30 minutes, or until the topping begins to brown.

DELISH LENTIL AND CAPER TRAYBAKE WITH MINT AND CHILLI YOGHURT

SERVES 4–6

Designed for comfort and ease, this is a satisfying throw-together meal for a relaxed weekday evening. This delightful array of simple wholefoods is a one-tray wonder for a quick lunch or dinner, and also happens to be one of my current favourite traybakes. I love the comfort of potato and kūmara, especially here, with the added burst of salty baked capers, pops of crunchy lentils, earthy cumin seeds and a touch of smoky essence. The finishing layers are the icing on the cake: dollops of refreshing, slightly spicy mint yoghurt, a scatter of fresh mint leaves and sliced creamy avocado to create the picture of simplicity, nutrition and deliciousness.

Preheat the oven to 180°C (350°F) fan-bake. Line a large baking tray with baking paper.

Place all the traybake ingredients in a large bowl and toss until well combined. Tip onto the prepared tray and spread out evenly. Bake for about 50 minutes, or until the veggies are just tender and golden brown.

For the Mint and chilli yoghurt, place all the ingredients in a bowl and mix to combine. Place in the fridge to firm up while the traybake is in the oven.

To serve, remove the tray from the oven and top with sliced avocado and fresh mint leaves. Finish with a drizzle of Mint and chilli yoghurt and a handful of microgreens, if using. Serve the remaining yoghurt on the side.

TRAYBAKE

2 kūmara, cut into batons
2 medium–large agria potatoes, cut into bite-sized cubes
½ head cauliflower, cut into bite-sized florets (about 3–4 packed cups)
400 g (14 oz) can brown lentils, drained and rinsed, or 1½ cups cooked lentils
1 large red capsicum, sliced lengthways into strips
⅓ cup capers, drained
1 red onion, finely sliced
2 cloves garlic, finely chopped
3 tablespoons pumpkin seeds
1½ tablespoons olive oil
1½ teaspoons smoked paprika
1 teaspoon cumin seeds
¾ teaspoon mixed spice
1 teaspoon sea salt

MINT AND CHILLI YOGHURT

⅔ cup coconut yoghurt
¼ cup lime juice
1 clove garlic, crushed or finely grated
1 packed tablespoon finely chopped fresh mint leaves
2 teaspoons pure maple syrup
⅛ teaspoon chilli flakes

TO SERVE (OPTIONAL)

sliced avocado
fresh mint leaves
microgreens

WINTER WELLNESS CURRIED BUTTERNUT AND KŪMARA SOUP WITH GARLIC FENNEL FLATBREAD

SERVES 4–6

SOUP
- olive or avocado oil (optional)
- 2 brown onions, diced
- about 16 cloves of garlic, peeled
- 2 tablespoons finely chopped fresh ginger
- 1 kg (2 lb 4 oz) butternut pumpkin, peeled, deseeded and diced
- 1 medium–large purple kūmara, peeled and diced
- 1 granny smith apple, peeled, cored and diced
- 4 cups water
- 1½ tablespoons pure maple syrup
- 2 tablespoons mild curry powder
- 1 tablespoon ground cinnamon
- 1 teaspoon ground cumin
- 1 teaspoon ground turmeric
- ½ teaspoon ground nutmeg
- ½ teaspoon ground ginger
- ¼ teaspoon ground pepper
- 1 teaspoon sea salt
- 400 ml (14 fl oz) can coconut cream

GARLIC FENNEL FLATBREAD
- 1 cup chickpea flour (besan)
- 1 teaspoon garlic powder
- ¼ teaspoon sea salt
- 1 teaspoon olive oil
- ¾ cup water
- ½ teaspoon fennel seeds
- 1 large clove garlic, crushed or finely grated

I've been making this belly-warming soup for quite some time now. It's a wholesome blend of natural, healing ingredients including ginger, turmeric and a large quantity of garlic, along with creamy butternut pumpkin, kūmara, coconut cream and bright, punchy spices. This is a wonderful winter soup for the whole family. Naturally sweetened with a simple green apple and a dash of pure maple syrup, this large batch of soup comes together with ease and makes a beautiful lunch or dinner on a chilly day, especially when served with the very easy Garlic fennel flatbread. The soup can be stored in the freezer for at least 3 months.

Preheat the oven to 180°C (350°F) fan-bake. Line a baking tray with baking paper.

Heat the oil, if using, in a large frying pan over medium–high heat. Add the onion, garlic and ginger and cook for 5–7 minutes, stirring frequently, until soft and fragrant.

Transfer to a large saucepan along with all the other ingredients except for the coconut cream. Cover, bring to a boil, then simmer for about 30 minutes, or until the veggies are tender.

Transfer to a blender. You will need to do this in two batches. If your blender is not designed to blend hot liquid, let the soup cool slightly before blending. Blend until smooth and creamy. Alternatively, you can use a stick blender for this step. Transfer back to the saucepan and add the coconut cream reserving a little to garnish. Stir to combine well.

For the flatbread, whisk together the chickpea flour, garlic powder, salt, oil and water until all clumps are blended. Pour the batter onto the prepared tray and sprinkle over the fennel seeds and fresh garlic. Bake for 20–25 minutes, or until golden with crispy edges.

To serve, pour the soup evenly into bowls and garnish with coconut cream, herbs and pepper. Serve the flatbread on the side.

Tip: *This flatbread also works well as a pizza base. Simply cook, then add your favourite toppings.*

SERVES 4

TERIYAKI TOFU POKE BOWLS

1–1½ cups brown rice (see tip)
2–3 cups water (see tip)
600 g (1 lb 5 oz) organic firm tofu, drained and diced
¾ cup diced telegraph cucumber
½ capsicum, finely diced
2 large avocados, stoned and diced or sliced
3 tablespoons pine nuts
1 tablespoon black sesame seeds

TERIYAKI SAUCE
¼ cup tamari
3 tablespoons water
2 tablespoons apple cider vinegar
2½ tablespoons pure maple syrup
2 cloves garlic, crushed or finely grated
1 teaspoon sesame oil
1 teaspoon garlic granules

TO SERVE (OPTIONAL)
pickled ginger
julienned carrot
nori strips
vegan mayo
lime wedges

These sushi-inspired bowls are a long-time favourite of my children – even little Jai. Eli and Milo enjoy cooking this recipe and preparing the bowls creatively for an easy, protein-packed meal loaded with nutritional elements. We've been making this meal for a number of years now, and over time Eli has perfected the teriyaki marinade and made it his very own signature recipe. The inspiration originated from our precious family travels in a popular French town, Soorts-Hossegor. If you've ever eaten good sushi in Hossegor, you'll know the bowls I'm talking about. A big shout-out to CJ Sushi; it's a must-visit if you're ever in the region!

Preheat the oven to 200°C (400°F) fan-bake. Line a baking tray with baking paper.

Place the rice and water in a saucepan, cover, and bring to a boil. Reduce heat and simmer for about 25 minutes, or until the water has absorbed and the rice is soft.

For the Teriyaki sauce, place all the ingredients in a bowl and whisk to combine.

Heat a large non-stick frying pan over medium–high heat. Add the tofu and Teriyaki sauce and cook for about 1 minute, or until the sauce begins to bubble. Reduce heat and simmer, stirring occasionally, for about 10 minutes.

At this point, the tofu is ready to serve. However, for a firmer, slightly crispy texture, transfer to the prepared tray along with any excess sauce from the pan. Spread out evenly. Bake for about 15–18 minutes, or until the tofu is beginning to crisp around the edges.

To serve, divide the rice evenly between four bowls, followed by the cucumber, capsicum and tofu. Top with avocado, pine nuts and sesame seeds. Add any other toppings, such as pickled ginger, carrot, nori strips, vegan mayo and lime wedges.

Tip: *1 cup of rice is based on the standard serving size of ½ cup cooked rice per person. For a larger meal, cook 1½ cups rice to 3 cups of water – we usually do.*

TANDOORI CAULIFLOWER, JACKFRUIT AND CHICKPEA BOWLS WITH CREAMY INDIAN RAITA

SERVES 4

½ head cauliflower (about 500 g/1 lb 2 oz), cut into large florets then finely sliced
400 g (14 oz) can young jackfruit, drained
400 g (14 oz) can chickpeas, drained and rinsed (or 1½ cups cooked chickpeas)
½ cup coconut yoghurt
3 tablespoons pure maple syrup
1 tablespoon lime zest
1 tablespoon lime juice
1¼ teaspoons ground coriander
1 teaspoon paprika
1 teaspoon ground cumin
1 teaspoon garlic powder
1 teaspoon onion powder
½ teaspoon ground turmeric
½ teaspoon ground ginger
1 teaspoon sea salt
pinch cayenne pepper (optional)
1½ cups Indian Raita (page 241)

TO SERVE (OPTIONAL)
sprouts (radish, pea, sunflower, alfalfa, etc.)
garden greens (spinach, kale, rocket, etc.)
sliced avocado
brown rice (optional)

There is definitely something special about baking cauliflower, chickpeas and jackfruit together. The neutral taste and textures of the trio create a perfectly balanced canvas to experiment with. If you enjoy bold flavours, like me, this is definitely for you. The sweetly spiced tandoori mix is matched like a dream with the refreshing yoghurt raita, then constructed into a yummy nourish bowl alongside fresh avocado and your fave greens. These Indian-inspired aromas will linger in your kitchen for a while. The wholesome combo can also be served in dosas, or even in tacos and burritos, to create a fun fiesta for friends and family.

Preheat the oven to 180°C (350°F) fan-bake. Line a baking tray with baking paper.

Place all the ingredients in a large bowl and toss to combine, ensuring everything is evenly coated in the spices. Tip onto the prepared tray and spread out evenly. Bake for about 30–35 minutes, tossing once or twice, until cauliflower is tender and beginning to crisp.

To serve, divide the tandoori mixture evenly between four bowls, followed by a large handful of fresh sprouts or greens and avocado. Finish with even dollops of the Indian Raita, and serve with rice, if desired.

SERVES 4

SAN CLEMENTE TURMERIC TOFU AND CHICKPEA SCRAMBLE BOWLS

⅔ cup quinoa (or gluten-free grain of choice)

1⅓ cups water

4 cups baby rocket leaves (or baby spinach)

2 cups cherry tomatoes, halved

2 large avocados, stoned and sliced

1 cup Moroccan Chermoula (page 246)

TURMERIC TOFU AND CHICKPEA SCRAMBLE

400 g (14 oz) can chickpeas drained and rinsed (or 1½ cups cooked chickpeas)

300 g (10½ oz) organic tofu

2 small spring onions, finely sliced

½ teaspoon ground turmeric

½ teaspoon sea salt

⅛ teaspoon ground black pepper

1 teaspoon sesame oil

2 cloves garlic, finely chopped

1 tablespoon tamari

TO SERVE (OPTIONAL)

Roast Garlic Dressing (page 256) or Hemp Miso Aioli (page 252)

microgreens

cracked pepper

chilli flakes

The San Clemente bowl was born from Ricardo's years of travel. Whenever he flew to California to compete in a surf contest, he would devour numerous bowls similar to this one. The boys and I joined him on a trip one year and we spent a wonderful month together in San Clemente, a beachside city in Orange County. Among other fun adventures, we finally had the opportunity to enjoy the vegan bowls he'd been raving about for years! This protein-packed bowl can be enjoyed for any meal; breakfast, brunch, lunch or dinner, and is super-quick and easy to put together. The tasty scramble takes no more than 10 minutes and is also excellent served in gluten-free wraps, lettuce cups and sandwiches for lunch.

Place the quinoa and water in a saucepan, cover and bring to a boil. Once boiling, reduce the heat to low and simmer for 12–15 minutes, or until the water has absorbed and the quinoa is soft and fluffy.

For the scramble, place the chickpeas in a large bowl and mash until semi-smooth, leaving a few small chunks and whole chickpeas for texture. Using your hands, lightly crumble the tofu into the chickpeas, leaving large chunks for texture. Add the spring onion, turmeric, salt and pepper, and gently toss through to evenly combine.

Heat the sesame oil in a large pan over medium–high heat. Add the garlic and cook for 2–3 minutes, tossing frequently until golden and fragrant. Add the tofu and chickpea mixture along with the tamari and cook, tossing frequently, for about 3–4 minutes until heated through.

To serve, divide the quinoa, Turmeric tofu and chickpea scramble and remaining ingredients between four shallow bowls, finishing each with a dollop of Moroccan Chermoula and a drizzle of Roast Garlic Dressing or Hemp Miso Aioli, if using. Garnish with microgreens and cracked pepper or chilli flakes.

MOROCCAN KŪMARA NUGGETS WITH WHOLESOME HEMPSEED TABOULI

MAKES 20 NUGGETS
SERVES 3–4

You can count on this meal for multiple reasons: it's easy, delicious, not too heavy, not too light and really nutritious. I really enjoyed creating these simple nuggets using a combination of orange and purple kūmara. With a beautiful light and fluffy texture, they're so lovely to snack on and great for little lunch boxes, too. The raw hempseed tabouli comes together in about five minutes and will happily sit alongside any dish for a highly nutritious and revitalising bite. Hempseeds are a great source of complete protein, as well as boasting essential fatty acids, magnesium, calcium, iron, potassium, vitamin E and zinc – they're a true superfood.

Bring a saucepan half-filled with water to a boil. Place the kūmara in a colander over the water, cover, and steam for 15 minutes, or until just tender.

Preheat the oven to 180°C (350°F) fan-bake. Line a baking tray with baking paper.

Add the kūmara and chickpeas to a large bowl and mash until mostly smooth, leaving a few whole chickpeas and small chunks of kūmara for texture.

Add all remaining nugget ingredients except cinnamon and hempseeds or sesame seeds, and mix to combine. Using your hands, shape the mixture into 20 rectangular or oval nuggets. Place each nugget on the prepared tray and lightly sprinkle with cinnamon and hempseeds or sesame seeds, if desired. Bake for about 35 minutes, or until golden and slightly crispy.

For the Hempseed tabouli, place all the ingredients in a large bowl and toss to combine.

To serve, divide the nuggets evenly between four shallow bowls. Add a serving of Hempseed tabouli and sliced avocado. Garnish with a sprinkle of pomegranate seeds for a pop of colour, if desired.

500 g (1 lb 2 oz) kūmara, peeled (I use a combination of orange and purple)
2 x 400 g (14 oz) cans chickpeas, drained and rinsed (or 3 cups cooked chickpeas)
½ cup almond meal (ground almonds)
handful fresh parsley, finely chopped
2 spring onions, finely sliced
⅓ cup pitted black olives, sliced
¼ cup chopped pistachios (or almonds)
2 teaspoons ground cumin
1 teaspoon sea salt
½ teaspoon ground coriander
½ teaspoon mixed spice
⅛ teaspoon ground white pepper
sprinkle of ground cinnamon
sprinkle of hempseeds or sesame seeds (optional)

HEMPSEED TABOULI
1 cup hempseeds
1 cup finely chopped fresh parsley
handful fresh mint, finely chopped
½ cup finely diced telegraph cucumber
½ cup finely diced red onion
1 cup finely diced tomato
2 tablespoons lemon juice
1 teaspoon lemon zest
½ teaspoon sea salt

MEDITERRANEAN RATATOUILLE MINGLE WITH THYME AND CUMIN HUMMUS

SERVES 4–6

4 medium–large agria potatoes, cut into cubes and/or wedges
2 red capsicums, sliced lengthways into strips
2 zucchini, cut into rounds
1 eggplant, cut into bite-sized cubes
4 cloves garlic, crushed or finely grated
1 cup pitted black olives, halved lengthways
1 cup chopped fresh parsley
12 pitted dried dates, finely chopped
2 packed tablespoons lemon zest
2 tablespoons dried oregano
2 teaspoons ground cumin
1 teaspoon caraway seeds
2 tablespoons balsamic vinegar
2 tablespoons olive oil
1½ tablespoons pure maple syrup
1½ teaspoons sea salt
1 cup tomato passata
1½–2 tablespoons buckwheat flour

TO SERVE
¼ cup sliced sun-dried tomatoes
¼–½ teaspoon chilli flakes
handful fresh dill, chopped
1½ cups Cumin and Thyme Hummus (page 244) or store-bought hummus

This earthy traybake makes an effortless and flavoursome mingle – simply toss the ingredients in a bowl and bake. The ratatouille makes a large batch and can be made in advance and kept refrigerated. Its flavours will improve with time and make for a wondrous lunch or dinner over the following days. If you have the extra time, especially as the ratatouille bakes, be sure to whip up the Cumin and Thyme Hummus (page 244) and spoon a few generous dollops of it over the ratatouille before serving. Alternatively, serve with any natural store-bought hummus.

Preheat the oven to 180°C (350°F) fan-bake. Line two large baking trays with baking paper.

Place all the ingredients – but only half of the parsley – in an extra-large bowl. If you don't have a bowl large enough, you will need to use two. Toss until combined and evenly coated.

Divide the vegetable mixture between prepared trays and spread out evenly. Bake for about 50 minutes. Halfway through the cooking time, swap the trays around from top to bottom and toss the veggies on the tray. Continue cooking until the veggies are tender and golden brown.

To serve, transfer the vegetables to a large serving platter. Gently toss through the remaining parsley. Top with the sun-dried tomato, chilli flakes, fresh dill and a few dollops of hummus. Serve any remaining hummus on the side.

SERVES 4

CREAMY HARISSA PEANUT SATAY NOODLES

250 g (9 oz) gluten-free spaghetti noodles (I use brown rice or quinoa pasta)
1 teaspoon olive or avocado oil (optional)
1 red onion, diced
3 spring onions, finely sliced
3 cloves garlic, finely chopped
1 tablespoon finely chopped or grated fresh ginger
1 carrot, julienned
1 large green capsicum, finely sliced
1 cup sugar snap peas, trimmed
1 cup frozen edamame beans, thawed
3 cups fresh spinach, roughly chopped
2 teaspoons rose harissa paste to taste (see note page 34)

SATAY SAUCE
½ cup smooth peanut butter
½ cup canned coconut milk
¼ cup lime juice
3½ tablespoons tamari
2 tablespoons pure maple syrup
1 tablespoon rice vinegar
2 cloves garlic

TO SERVE
1 tablespoon black sesame seeds
fresh coriander leaves

These creamy peanut noodles make the perfect midweek meal. They are full of lightly cooked, crunchy veggies and smothered in the creamiest satay sauce, with a touch of harissa for that sweetly spiced mouthful. Although I love the combination of these flavours as they are, the great thing about this dish (and the same goes for many of my recipes) is that you can adjust the flavours to suit your palate. If you desire a bold, salty flavour, add a little more tamari. For more spice, add a little more harissa paste. For more sweetness, add a touch more maple syrup.

Bring a large saucepan of water to a boil. Add the noodles and cook according to the packet instructions (usually about 10–15 minutes).

For the Satay sauce, place all the ingredients in a blender and blend for about 20–30 seconds, or until smooth.

Heat the oil, if using, in a large frying pan or wok over medium-high heat. Add the onions, garlic and ginger and cook for about 5–7 minutes, stirring frequently, until soft and fragrant. Add the carrot, capsicum and sugar snap peas, and continue to cook for 3–4 minutes, or until the veggies are just tender. Add the edamame beans and spinach and cook for a further 1–2 minutes.

Add the Satay sauce, harissa and drained noodles to the vegetables and gently mix through.

To serve, sprinkle over the sesame seeds and fresh coriander leaves.

SERVES 4

WHOLESOME CHINESE-STYLE ROAST CASHEW RED RICE

1¼ cups raw cashews
1 cup red, black or brown rice
2 cups water
2 teaspoons sesame oil (optional)
5 spring onions, finely sliced
3 cloves garlic, finely chopped
1 cup finely shredded red cabbage
1 carrot, julienned
1 red capsicum, finely sliced
1 bunch bok choy, roughly chopped
½ cup frozen peas (or edamame)
½ teaspoon Chinese five spice
1 tablespoon white miso paste
2 tablespoons water
2½ tablespoons tamari
1 tablespoon rice wine vinegar (or an extra tablespoon water)
¾ cup mung bean sprouts

TO SERVE (OPTIONAL)
fresh coriander leaves

This is a quick and easy, healthy version of the traditional Chinese fried rice. It encompasses many elements of nutrition and includes the added benefits of red rice – a gluten-free wholegrain enriched with antioxidants and magnesium – along with crunchy roast cashews and rainbow veggies. I like to keep the mung beans raw in this recipe as I love their contrasting, refreshing crunch. This simple throw-together can be enjoyed either hot or cold, served with lots of fresh coriander. We often top our bowls with sliced avocado, too.

Preheat the oven to 180°C (350°F) fan-bake. Line a baking tray with baking paper.

Place the cashews on the prepared tray and spread out evenly. Bake for about 8 minutes, or until golden. Watch closely as they can burn quickly. Set aside.

Place the rice and water in a saucepan, cover and bring to a boil. Reduce heat and simmer for about 25 minutes, or until the water has absorbed and the rice is soft.

Heat the oil, if using, in a large frying pan or wok over medium–high heat. Add the spring onion and garlic and cook for about 3–5 minutes, stirring frequently, until soft and fragrant. Add the cabbage, carrot, capsicum, bok choy, frozen peas and Chinese five spice, and continue to cook for 4–5 minutes, or until the veggies are just tender.

Add the rice, miso paste, water, tamari, rice vinegar and ¾ of a cup of the roast cashews (reserve the rest for serving). Toss to combine everything together and cook for a further minute.

To serve, mix through the mung bean sprouts and scatter over the remaining cashews. Finish by topping with fresh coriander leaves.

MAKES 6 PATTIES

EPIC PLANT-BASED BURGER PATTIES WITH QUICK AVOCADO MAYO

1 teaspoon olive or avocado oil (optional), plus extra for frying
1 brown onion, finely diced
400 g (14 oz) can kidney beans, drained and rinsed (or 1½ cups cooked kidney beans)
400 g (14 oz) can chickpeas, drained and rinsed (or 1½ cups cooked chickpeas)
handful fresh coriander, finely chopped
3 tablespoons almond meal (ground almonds)
2 tablespoons nutritional yeast
1 teaspoon onion powder
1 teaspoon garlic powder
1 teaspoon ground cumin
1 teaspoon paprika
1 teaspoon sea salt
¼ teaspoon smoked paprika

TO SERVE (OPTIONAL)
gluten-free buns
lettuce leaves
portobello mushrooms
sliced avocado
sliced tomato
sliced red onion
sliced cucumber
sprouts
Avocado Mayo (page 249)

I personally love these patties served with fresh greens and a generous dollop of the creamy Avocado Mayo (page 249), but according to the boys they are also really good slabbed between a burger bun. Nutritious, flavourful and so quick and simple to make, these lovely, luscious patties are a delicious weekday idea for the whole family, served however you please. The beautiful Avocado Mayo is an easy, wholesome dressing that will complement any dish.

Heat the oil, if using, in a large frying pan over medium–high heat. Add the onion and cook for about 5–7 minutes, stirring frequently, until soft and fragrant.

Put the kidney beans and chickpeas in a large bowl. Mash with a fork or potato masher until mostly smooth, with a few chunks remaining for texture.

Add the onion and all other ingredients to the bowl and mix to combine.

Using your hands, shape the mixture into 6 burger patties (each patty should be about 2–2½ cm/¾–1 in thick). Arrange the patties on a plate and freeze for about 30 minutes, or until firm.

To heat the patties, put a dash of olive or avocado oil in a large non-stick frying pan over medium–high heat. Once hot, reduce heat to medium–low.

Place half of the patties in the pan and cook for about 3 minutes, until golden. Gently flip and cook the other side for another 3 minutes. Carefully remove and place on a paper towel to absorb any excess oil. Repeat with the remaining patties.

To serve, build a burger using a gluten-free bun, lettuce leaves or portobello mushrooms. Add your favourite toppings, such as sliced avocado, tomato, red onion, cucumber and sprouts, and a few generous dollops of the Avocado Mayo. You could also serve the patties over a fresh green salad.

Tip: *When the patties are heated, they will soften, so ensure they're handled carefully.*

WALNUT AND CAULIFLOWER 'CHORIZO' TACOS WITH PINEAPPLE SALSA

SERVES 4–6

These easy tacos are a delightful mouthful of fresh and flavourful ingredients. The slightly smoky chorizo-style mingle creates a healthy taco filler that can be served without heating for a completely raw meal using lettuce leaves as the taco base. Hosting a combination of fresh, sweet and spicy, the ultra-light, juicy salsa will be a fabulous contrasting addition to your taco fiesta! This wholesome combo can also be used to create satisfying burritos.

For the Pineapple salsa, place all the ingredients in a bowl and toss to combine. Cover and place in the fridge until needed.

For the 'Chorizo' filling, place all the ingredients in a large food processor and pulse for about 6–8 seconds to a crumbly texture. Be careful not to over-process or the mixture will lose its texture. Remove the blade from the blender and mix the ingredients, if needed, to ensure everything is well combined.

The filling is ready to serve raw if desired. To serve warm, heat a large frying pan over medium–high heat. Add the mixture and cook for about 5 minutes, tossing frequently, until warmed through.

To serve, remove the Pineapple salsa from the fridge and place on the table alongside the other elements of the meal so everyone can create their own tacos (or burritos). We like to start with the 'Chorizo' filling, followed by the Pineapple salsa and finish with diced avocado and a drizzle of aioli.

Tip: *Be cautious when purchasing the soft tortillas sold in supermarkets as they are often full of additives. The tortillas featured in this recipe are our family go-to. They're 100 per cent naturally grown soft corn tacos made by our lovely local friends at La Tortilla Shop. I also have a super-easy chickpea taco recipe in my first cookbook, Raw & Free.*

PINEAPPLE SALSA
2 cups finely diced fresh pineapple
1 red capsicum, finely diced
¼ cup finely diced red onion
¾ cup fresh coriander, finely chopped
1 tablespoon lime juice
1 clove garlic, crushed or finely grated
¾ teaspoon sea salt
½ teaspoon ground cumin

'CHORIZO' FILLING
½ small head cauliflower (about 450 g/1 lb)
1 cup walnuts
handful fresh parsley
¼ cup nutritional yeast
3 tablespoons coconut sugar
2½ tablespoons tomato paste
1 small clove garlic
2 teaspoons onion powder
2 teaspoons smoked paprika
1 tablespoon dried oregano
1 teaspoon dried thyme
1 teaspoon sea salt

TO SERVE
natural soft tortillas (see tip)
diced avocado
vegan aioli (optional)

SERVES 4–6

MEXICAN KŪMARA WEDGES WITH HEARTY BLACK BEAN GUACAMOLE SALAD

4 medium purple kūmara, cut into wedges
½–1 tablespoon olive oil (optional)
1 teaspoon garlic powder
1 teaspoon onion powder
1 teaspoon smoked paprika
1 teaspoon cumin seeds
1 teaspoon dried herbs (sweet basil, oregano or mixed herbs)
sea salt and cracked pepper, to taste
400 g (14 oz) can black beans, drained and rinsed (or 1½ cups cooked black beans)
2 cups finely chopped cos lettuce
handful fresh basil, roughly chopped
handful fresh coriander, roughly chopped
½ cup corn kernels
1 red capsicum, finely diced
1 cup cherry tomatoes, diced
2 spring onions, finely sliced
½ small red onion, finely diced
½ cup pitted green olives, sliced
lime wedges, to serve

GUACAMOLE DRESSING

2 large avocados, stoned and peeled
2 tablespoons lime juice
2 tablespoons coconut yoghurt
1 clove garlic, crushed or finely grated
½ teaspoon sea salt
⅛ teaspoon ground white pepper

When it comes to simple and nutritious meals, this wholesome bowl is almost unbeatable. The generous black bean guacamole salad is seriously good – I once shared a similar version of this recipe on my Instagram, @rawandfree, and it went bananas! This must-try recipe comes together with ease and creates an impressive bowlful of nutrition. If you prefer potato wedges, feel free to replace the kūmara with agria potatoes.

Preheat the oven to 180°C (350°F) fan-bake. Line a large baking tray with baking paper.

For the wedges, place the kūmara, oil, if using, garlic powder, onion powder, smoked paprika, cumin seeds and dried herbs in a large bowl. Season to taste and toss to evenly coat the wedges in the seasoning. Place on the prepared tray and spread out in a single layer (use two trays if need be). Bake for about 45 minutes, tossing once or twice, or until golden and crispy around the edges.

For the Guacamole dressing, place all the ingredients in a bowl and mash together with a fork until smooth and creamy.

To make the salad, put the black beans in a large bowl with the lettuce, basil, coriander, corn, capsicum, tomato, spring onion, red onion and olives. Add the Guacamole dressing and mix to combine.

To serve, divide the kūmara wedges and guacamole salad between shallow bowls. Arrange the lime wedges at the side of each bowl.

SERVES 4

GREEN GOODNESS BOWLS WITH BALSAMIC TURMERIC CHICKPEAS AND HERBY MISO DRESSING

1–1½ cups black rice (see tip)
2–3 cups water (see tip)

BALSAMIC TURMERIC CHICKPEAS
2 x 400 g (14 oz) cans chickpeas, drained and rinsed (or 3 cups cooked chickpeas)
4 teaspoons balsamic vinegar
1 tablespoon pure maple syrup
1½ teaspoons garlic powder
½ teaspoon ground turmeric
¾ teaspoon sea salt
⅛ tablespoon ground white pepper
1 teaspoon olive or avocado oil (optional)

HERBY MISO DRESSING (SEE TIPS)
¾ cup raw cashews
handful each fresh spinach, coriander and parsley
2 tablespoons white miso paste
1 tablespoon wholegrain mustard
2 tablespoons lemon juice
2 small cloves garlic
2 teaspoons pure maple syrup
1 teaspoon tamari
½ teaspoon apple cider vinegar

GREENS PER BOWL
1 cup fresh greens (spinach, rocket, microgreens, etc.)
¼ cup frozen edamame beans, thawed
½ avocado, stoned and sliced
telegraph cucumber ribbons
1 tablespoon hempseeds
1 tablespoon pumpkin seeds

Eating more greens is easy with these dreamy, wholesome bowls. Not only are they super-simple and quick to throw together, but they also create a delicious, healthful meal with a multitude of nutritional benefits. With a gorgeous vibrancy and beautiful, bold flavours, the Balsamic turmeric chickpeas stand out among the greens, and pair perfectly with the delish Herby miso dressing. Fee free to mix up the fresh greens and gluten-free wholegrains with whatever you have on hand.

Place the rice and water in a saucepan, cover, and bring to a boil. Reduce heat and simmer for about 25–30 minutes, or until the water has absorbed and the rice is soft.

For the Herby miso dressing, place all the ingredients in a blender and blend until smooth and creamy. Set aside.

For the chickpeas, place all the ingredients except the oil in a large bowl and toss until the chickpeas are evenly coated. Heat the oil, if using, in a large non-stick frying pan over medium heat. Add the chickpeas and any remaining marinade and cook for about 8 minutes, tossing frequently, until all the liquid has absorbed into the chickpeas.

To serve, divide the rice evenly between four bowls, followed by the chickpeas. Arrange the greens, edamame, avocado and cucumber, if using, in each of the bowls, sprinkle with hempseeds and pumpkin seeds and serve with a generous drizzle of Herby miso dressing. Serve with any remaining dressing on the side.

Tips: 1 cup of rice is based on the standard serving size of ½ cup cooked rice per person. For a larger meal, cook 1½ cups rice to 3 cups of water.

This dressing also works well warmed and mixed through gluten-free pasta. Store any leftover dressing in the fridge for up to 5 days.

WHOLEFOOD SNACKS AND LUNCH BOXES

WHOLEFOOD SNACKS AND LUNCH BOXES

I live with several hungry (and often fussy) boys of all ages who are very physically active, so I understand the necessity of having plenty of quick and healthy snacks on hand. While I fully appreciate the natural wholefood alternatives becoming increasingly available, like many, I'm aware that the majority of the highly processed and extremely addictive packaged 'foods' so heavily promoted on supermarket shelves are overflowing with unwanted additives and offer very little nutritional value. Although these items are a convenient option (I'm a busy mum; I get it!), this toxic-chemical-laden junk is formulated to exploit our primal cravings for salt and sugar, and when consumed daily over the long-term, it can cause serious harm throughout the body.

On top of that, pre-packaged foods drive the heavy demand for plastic packaging, which we all know has negative effects on our environment. I strongly believe it's of fundamental importance for our overall health and longevity to consciously avoid these foods, with their refined sugars and carbohydrates, and embrace nature's nutrient-dense, ready-to-go foods, which include sustainably grown wholefoods such as fresh fruits, veggies, nuts and seeds.

So, where do we start?

A wonderful place to begin is with a complete kitchen makeover! Clean out *all* packaged items featuring unusual names and numbers (likely printed on the back of the packet) and adopt a new rule of thumb: always read the label on packaging before purchasing.

I'm not suggesting every packaged item is a no-go — now more than ever there are some excellent natural snacks available, along with daily wholefood staples. I'm also not saying that a fun treat is out of the question (my big boys definitely enjoy treating themselves at the dairy from time to time) but removing the majority of the unhealthy items from your home will help you and your family avoid using these foods as your primary source of fuel. Remember: it's not what we do occasionally, but what we do each day that has the long-term positive or negative effects on our overall health.

Once your kitchen is cleansed and refreshed, it's time to restock with plenty of healthful options, such as fresh fruits, dried fruit, produce, nuts and seeds (see my additional list of ideas below). This change may feel a little abrupt or even unsettling to begin with, and you can probably expect a few grumpy reactions from the little (or big!) people in your home, but trust me, your family will benefit tremendously and adapt more quickly than you may think. Tastebuds will adjust (this doesn't take long) and hopefully you'll enjoy making and eating the nutritious recipes in this chapter.

Simple wholefood snack ideas and lunch box fillers

The recipes in this chapter focus on wholesome lunch box ideas, light bites for inbetween meals and even a few sneaky breakfast options. Before you dive in, here's a list of simple, natural snack ideas for every day. With a little preparation, planning and commitment, it can be easier to make healthier choices that take advantage of the delicious foods readily available in nature (see over page).

- Plenty of fresh fruit: Let Mother Nature be your guide and enjoy all of the seasonal fruits on offer – I bet there are some you have yet to try!
- Frozen fruit: a key smoothie ingredient. My youngest, Jai, also enjoys a small bowlful of frozen fruits, such as berries and mangos.
- Freshly squeezed fruit or veggie juice.
- Smoothies and smoothie bowls: smoothies are our go-to any time of the day – see Chapter 1 for a refresher.
- Homemade ice blocks. A handy tip is to pour any leftover smoothies into an ice-block mould and freeze.
- Homemade organic popcorn.
- Chia pudding.
- Coconut yoghurt and fresh fruit: add a drizzle of pure maple syrup for a delish treat.
- Homemade bliss balls.
- Wholefood energy bars (page 225).
- Homemade wholefood cookies (page 220).
- Homemade muffins.
- Hummus (page 224) and wholefood crackers (page 200).
- Dehydrated fruit or crackers.
- Guacamole and veggie sticks.
- Frozen medjool dates stuffed with nut butter.
- Dried fruit (sulphur- and preservative-free): raisins, apricots and figs are my favourites.
- Wholesome trail mix of nuts and seeds (page 204).
- Leafy green wraps: lettuce, kale, spinach, collard or cabbage leaves work well. I use leaves religiously as a bread replacement; it's a great way to eat more greens, too.
- Rice paper veggie wraps.
- Homemade kūmara or potato wedges (pages 110, 170 and 182).
- Baked chickpeas.
- Kale chips (page 203).

Ideas for snacks or lunch box treats throughout this book include:

- Smoothies and smoothie bowls (see chapter 1).
- Dips (see chapter 5).
- Moroccan Kūmara Nuggets (see page 169).
- Quinoa and Lentil Balls (see page 144).
- Maple Mustard Potato (see page 80).
- Garlic Fennel Flatbread (see page 158).
- Coconut Bakon (see page 102).
- Turmeric Tofu and Chickpea Scramble (page 166).
- Smoky Spinach Cream Cheese Smashed Potatoes (page 149 – these can be made into bite-sized snacks).
- Mexican Kūmara Wedges (page 182).
- Wholesome Double-chocolate Chia Parfaits (page 291).

SERVES 3

MEDITERRANEAN SMASHED CHICKPEA SANDWICH FILLER

400 g (14 oz) can chickpeas, drained and rinsed (or 1½ cups cooked chickpeas)
¼ cup finely chopped fresh parsley
¼ cup finely diced red capsicum
6–8 pitted black or green olives, finely sliced
½ teaspoon onion powder
¼ teaspoon ground turmeric
2 tablespoons hulled tahini
2 tablespoons lemon juice
1 tablespoon pure maple syrup
1 tablespoon wholegrain mustard
sea salt and cracked pepper, to taste

TO SERVE (OPTIONAL)
lettuce or silverbeet cups
sliced spring onion
chilli flakes

I love the flavour combination of this easy egg-like mash, which can be put together in just five minutes. This recipe is a great one to make ahead and have in the fridge for a wholesome bite, ready to be dolloped into sandwiches or leafy green lettuce cups. Chickpeas are high in fibre, with a mild flavour and soft texture that makes them a versatile addition to many plant-based meals. You'll even find them in baked treats! They work well in this recipe as a mashed egg or tuna replacement.

Place the chickpeas in a bowl and mash with a fork, leaving a few small chunks.

Add the parsley, capsicum, olives, onion powder and turmeric, and toss to combine.

In a separate bowl, place the tahini, lemon juice, maple syrup and wholegrain mustard. Whisk until smooth.

Add the tahini mixture to the chickpeas, mix to combine then season to taste.

To serve, spoon into lettuce or silverbeet cups and top with spring onion and chilli flakes if desired. Any leftovers can be stored in a sealed container in the fridge for 3 to 5 days.

TASTY CORN AND SPINACH FRITTERS

MAKES 9 FRITTERS

1 cup chickpea flour (besan)
¾ cup water
¼ cup coconut yoghurt (see tip)
1 tablespoon chia seeds
½ teaspoon onion powder
½ teaspoon garlic powder
½ teaspoon sea salt
½ teaspoon baking powder
3 tablespoons nutritional yeast
1½ teaspoons ground cumin
1 teaspoon olive or avocado oil (optional), plus extra for frying
1 brown onion, sliced
2 cups fresh spinach
1 cup sweetcorn kernels

Who doesn't enjoy a good old corn fritter? Especially these delicious gluten-free ones, which have a few vibrant greens thrown into the mix. As good as they are, it's the versatility of these quick and easy fritters that I love the most. Whether I'm making them for lunch box fillers, after-school snacks, brunches, to serve as burger patties or even to partner with a wholesome salad, these tasty little fritters are a one-bowl wonder that work well for a no-fuss bite whatever the time of day.

In a large bowl, whisk together the chickpea flour, water and coconut yoghurt until all clumps in the batter are smoothed away. Add the chia seeds, onion powder, garlic powder, salt, baking powder, nutritional yeast and cumin and mix again. Set aside.

Heat the oil, if using, in a frying pan over medium–high heat. Add the onion and cook for 5–7 minutes, stirring frequently, until soft and fragrant. Add the spinach and cook for another minute, or until wilted.

Add the onion mixture to the batter along with the corn, then mix to combine.

Heat a dash of oil in a large, non-stick frying pan over low–medium heat. Once hot, add ¼-cup of the batter to the pan per fritter (I cook about three at a time) and cook for 3–4 minutes, or until bubbles form on the surface. Flip and cook for an additional 3–4 minutes, or until both sides are golden and crispy. Be careful not to have the heat up too high as the fritters will burn quickly.

Once cooked, transfer to a plate (keep this in the oven if you want to keep them warm) and repeat with the remaining batter. Serve.

Tip: *Use the thick layer of coconut yoghurt settled at the top half of the jar. Alternatively, you can use coconut cream.*

CHEESY CARROT AND CHIVE RAW OATMEAL BITES

MAKES 14 BITES

I created this recipe by complete fluke one day and was super-stoked with the outcome. With a tasty cheese and herb flavour, these savoury balls are excellent for sustained on-the-go energy, especially on those busy working weekdays. They work well as a savoury, nutritional bite in lunch boxes, too. I love that they're fully raw, quick and easy to prepare. They firm up with time in the fridge but still retain moisture from the naturally sweet and juicy carrots.

Place all the ingredients in a bowl and mix to combine, ensuring the tahini is evenly distributed throughout the mixture.

Using your hands, roll the mixture into about 14 balls.

Sprinkle the sesame seeds, if using, onto a large plate. Roll each ball through the coating.

Store in a sealed container in the fridge for 3–5 days.

3 cups grated carrots (about 3 carrots)
2 cups gluten-free rolled oats
1 bunch fresh chives, finely chopped
½ cup nutritional yeast
⅓ cup hulled tahini
⅓ cup raw cashews
¼ cup sunflower seeds
¼ cup melted coconut oil
1 tablespoon dried oregano
1 teaspoon ground paprika
¾ teaspoon sea salt
½ teaspoon fennel seeds

TO COAT (OPTIONAL)
¼ cup sesame seeds

MAKES ABOUT 45 CRACKERS

GLAZED BLACK RICE AND SESAME CRACKERS

⅓ cup black rice
1 cup water, plus 2 tablespoons water
2 tablespoons chia seeds
2 tablespoons olive oil
2 tablespoons tamari
1 cup almond meal (ground almonds)

TAMARI MISO GLAZE
2 tablespoons pure maple syrup
1 tablespoon water
1 tablespoon white miso paste
1 teaspoon tamari
2 teaspoons sesame seeds

I am often asked for healthy cracker ideas so I thought I would share this old family recipe. When we were little, my mum was ahead of the game in terms of natural, wholefood eating. A variation on these tasty crackers was one of the many homemade snacks she would pop in our lunch boxes. With the sweet miso and tamari glaze, they work as a flavourful grab-and-go nibble or school snack.

Place the rice in a saucepan with the cup of water then cover and bring to a boil. Reduce heat and simmer for about 25–30 minutes, or until the water has fully absorbed and the rice is soft. Remove the lid and let cool for 15 minutes.

Put the chia seeds and 2 tablespoons of water in a small bowl and whisk to combine. Let sit for 5–10 minutes to allow the mixture to thicken and form a gel. Once thickened, add the oil and tamari and mix to combine.

For the glaze, whisk all the ingredients in a bowl.

Place the cooked rice, almond meal and chia mixture in a food processor and pulse about 8 to 10 times, or until you have a semi-smooth dough-like texture with small pieces of black rice remaining. Divide the mixture in half and roll each into a ball.

Preheat the oven to 180°C (350°F) fan-bake. Line two baking trays with baking paper.

Line a clean surface with a large sheet of baking paper. Place one ball onto the sheet and cover with another sheet of baking paper. Evenly roll out about 3 mm (⅛ in) thick. Carefully peel off the top sheet. Use a small, about 3 cm (1¼ in) round, cookie cutter to cut circles. Gently peel these off and place on the prepared trays. Gather up the excess dough, knead again, then repeat the rolling and cutting. Repeat with the second ball of dough.

Brush each cracker with the miso glaze then bake for 15 minutes. Remove from the oven and reglaze each cracker. Reduce the heat to 100 °C (200°F) and bake for a further 45 minutes, glazing one more time, until lightly crispy. The crackers will firm up as they cool.

Let cool, then store in a sealed container for up to a week.

ELI'S CHEESY KALE CHIPS

SERVES 2–4

Eli, my gorgeous 15-year-old, would seriously eat these crunchy, cheesy flavoured greens every day if I made them – he's the first to acknowledge his obsession. Super-quick and easy to prepare, kale chips make a fabulous addition to everything, from lunch boxes to after-school snacks, nachos and pizzas toppers. They're also amazing thrown into pastas, salads and Buddha bowls, which is exactly the reason I included Eli's favourite simple recipe for you.

Preheat the oven to 180°C (350°F) fan-bake. Line a large baking tray with baking paper.

Place the kale and oil in a large bowl. Use your hands to massage the oil into the leaves for about a minute, or until they begin to soften. Add the nutritional yeast, season with salt, pepper or chilli flakes and massage the flavours into the leaves until evenly coated.

Transfer to prepared tray and spread out evenly. Bake for about 10–12 minutes, tossing frequently, until lightly crisp. Watch closely for the last few minutes as they can burn quickly. Serve immediately.

1 large bunch curly kale, stems removed, leaves roughly chopped
1 tablespoon olive oil
2–3 tablespoons nutritional yeast
¼–½ teaspoon sea salt, or to taste
cracked pepper or chilli flakes, to taste (optional)

MAKES 3½ CUPS

CARDAMOM-SPICED YOGHURT CHICKPEA TRAIL MIX

400 g (14 oz) can chickpeas, drained and rinsed (or 1½ cups cooked chickpeas)
1 cup sliced almonds
½ cup pumpkin seeds
½ cup sunflower seeds
¼ cup coconut yoghurt
1½ tablespoons tamari
1 heaped tablespoon lime zest
¼ teaspoon ground cardamom
1 teaspoon pure maple syrup
1 teaspoon garlic powder
⅓ cup raisins (optional)

Nuts and seeds coated in a creamy, cardamom-spiced yoghurt, then baked into a wholesome trail mix with a twist of crunchy chickpeas deliver an impressive snack to nibble on throughout the day. I enjoy this mingle with a large handful of raisins to add a bite of chewy sweetness to the mix, but you can omit them if you prefer a completely savoury mix.

Preheat the oven to 180°C (350°F) fan-bake. Line a large baking tray with baking paper.

Place the chickpeas, almonds and pumpkin and sunflower seeds in a bowl and toss to combine.

In a smaller bowl, mix the coconut yoghurt, tamari, lime zest, cardamom, maple syrup and garlic powder to combine. Add to the chickpea mixture and stir until everything is evenly coated.

Transfer to the prepared baking tray and spread out in a single layer. Bake, tossing once or twice, for about 25 minutes, or until golden and crunchy. Remove from the oven and mix through the raisins, if using.

Let cool completely before storing in a sealed jar for up to 5 days.

MAKES 1 LOAF

BEAUTIFULLY SPICED BANANA BREAD

1½ cups buckwheat flour
1 teaspoon baking powder
1 teaspoon baking soda
½ cup coconut sugar
1 tablespoon ground cinnamon
1 teaspoon ground ginger
½ teaspoon ground cardamom
¼ teaspoon ground nutmeg
1 cup rice milk (or other plant milk)
¼ cup melted coconut oil
1 teaspoon pure vanilla extract
2 cups very ripe bananas (about 4 bananas), mashed (see tip)
1 cup walnuts, roughly chopped
½ cup sultanas

TOPPING
1 small banana, sliced lengthways
1 tablespoon pure maple syrup

The aromas of this beautiful loaf will waft through your kitchen as it's baking in the oven and linger in your home for hours after. I love the soft, springy texture of this delightfully sweet bread. It has the perfect amount of aromatic spices to enhance the flavours, and a finishing touch of caramelised maple banana that really makes it sing. It's the perfect weekend loaf to enjoy with friends but is equally as good in a weekday lunch box.

Preheat the oven to 170°C (325°F) fan-bake. Line a loaf tin with baking paper.

Sift the buckwheat flour into a large bowl. Add the baking powder, baking soda, coconut sugar, cinnamon, ginger, cardamom and nutmeg. Mix to combine.

Make a well in the centre of the dry ingredients and add the rice milk, coconut oil and vanilla and mix to combine. Add the banana, walnuts and sultanas and mix again.

Tip the mixture into the prepared loaf tin and spread out evenly. Arrange the sliced banana on top and drizzle over the maple syrup.

Bake for 60–70 minutes, or until golden. To test if it's cooked through, insert a knife into the centre of the loaf. It should come out clean if the loaf is ready.

Remove from the tin and let cool before slicing and serving.

Store in a sealed container for 3–5 days.

Tip: *Ensure you use very ripe, spotty bananas in this recipe as they will really boost the natural flavour, texture and sweetness of the loaf.*

MAKES OVER 9 CUPS

GORGEOUS ALMOND BERRY GRANOLA

2 cups brown rice flakes (or gluten-free rolled oats)
2 cups sliced almonds
1 cup almonds
1 cup shredded coconut
½ teaspoon ground cardamom
½ teaspoon ground allspice
½ teaspoon sea salt
1 tablespoon pure vanilla extract
2 tablespoons coconut oil
¼ cup almond butter
¼ cup pure maple syrup
¾ cup dried cranberries
¾ cups freeze-dried raspberries (or strawberries or blueberries) (see tip)

TO SERVE (OPTIONAL)
coconut yoghurt
fresh fruit

This truly gorgeous almond granola boasts a divine selection of aromatic spices, and a touch of sweetness from the vivid, freeze-dried raspberries. Cardamom, a popular spice in Indian cuisine, has an array of complex flavours and is often described as fruity, citrusy and slightly minty. Here, it adds a lovely, subtle aroma to this beautiful granola. Feel free to use gluten-free rolled oats or mix things up with brown rice flakes for a crunchier texture. This satisfying granola is delish topped with coconut yoghurt and fresh berries, scattered over a smoothie bowl or simply eaten by the handful.

Preheat the oven to 160°C (315°F) fan-bake. Line a large baking tray with baking paper.

Place the rice flakes, sliced almonds, almonds, coconut, cardamom, allspice, salt and vanilla in a large bowl and toss to combine.

Heat a small saucepan over medium–high heat. Add the coconut oil, almond butter and maple syrup. Stir until the coconut oil is melted and the ingredients are combined. Add the melted mixture to the granola bowl and stir to combine.

Transfer the mixture to the prepared tray and spread out in a single layer. Bake for about 12–14 minutes, or until golden and crunchy. Watch closely for the last few minutes as it will burn quickly.

Let cool completely before breaking into small clusters. Mix through the cranberries and freeze-dried raspberries. Serve over fresh seasonal fruit with a dollop of coconut yoghurt, if desired.

Store in a sealed container for up to 2 weeks.

Tip: *Freeze-dried raspberries can be found in most health food stores. They really add to this granola, so they are worth getting. You can also use freeze-dried strawberries or blueberries in this recipe.*

FULLY LOADED PEAR AND SULTANA BIRDSEED BIRCHER

SERVES 4

A wholesome mix between a chia pudding and a bircher, this uber-vitalising, seedy blend is likely to become your new favourite breakfast or healthy snack idea. Fully loaded with many essential nutrients, it makes an excellent wholefood addition in lunch boxes and works perfectly as an energising breakfast or an on-the-go meal. This superfood blend makes a large batch that will last throughout the week. It can be efficiently heated on a chilly winter's day (but is equally as good eaten straight from the fridge). I would definitely add this to your repertoire for a healthful boost.

Place all the ingredients in a large bowl (or jar with a lid) and stir (or shake) vigorously to combine well. Let the mixture sit for a few minutes, then stir (or shake) again to ensure all the ingredients are well combined.

Place in the fridge for 1–2 hours to set, stirring occasionally.

To serve, place in a serving bowl or jar and top with fresh fruit, coconut yoghurt and mint, if desired.

Store in a sealed jar in the fridge for up to 3–5 days.

1 large ripe pear, peeled and grated
1½ cups brown rice flakes
3 cups rice milk (or other plant milk)
½ cup sultanas (or raisins)
¼ cup chia seeds
¼ cup pure maple syrup
3 tablespoons pumpkin seeds
3 tablespoons sunflower seeds
2 tablespoons hempseeds
2 tablespoons flaxseeds (linseeds)
2 teaspoons cacao powder
¾ teaspoon ground cinnamon
1 teaspoon pure vanilla extract

TO SERVE (OPTIONAL)
fresh fruit
coconut yoghurt
mint sprigs

MAKES 20–30 SNAPS

SUPERSEED SNAPS

2 cups pumpkin seeds
1 cup coconut flakes (coconut chips)
1 cup sliced almonds
¼ cup pure maple syrup
¼ cup hempseeds
¼ cup sesame seeds
2 tablespoons flaxseeds (linseeds)
2 tablespoons chia seeds
½ teaspoon pure vanilla extract
¼ teaspoon sea salt

This large batch of sweet and crunchy snaps was the very first recipe I created for this book! It was the tail end of summer, and my boys were competing in a surf contest one sunny morning, so I decided to trial a batch of these speedy, healthy snaps. I knew they were a hit when they were instantly devoured by everyone on the beach – of all ages! They're an easy energy booster loaded with simple seeds, coconut chips and sliced almonds, making them the perfect wholesome snack, lunch box addition or after-dinner bite.

Preheat the oven to 180°C (350°F) fan-bake. Line a large baking dish with baking paper. (I used a 38 cm x 25 cm (15 in x 10 in) dish).

Place all the ingredients in a bowl and toss until everything is combined and evenly coated in the maple syrup.

Transfer the mixture to the prepared dish and spread out evenly. Using the back of a spoon, press firmly over the mixture to pack it down. Bake for about 15 minutes, or until golden.

Remove from the oven and let cool completely. This is an important step that is going to help it bind together. It will crumble if not left to cool completely. When cool, snap into pieces of your desired shape and size.

Store in a sealed container for up to 7 days.

PEANUT BUTTER KŪMARA FUDGE BITES

MAKES 24 BITES

1 large purple kūmara (about 350–400 g/12–14 oz), peeled and diced
¾ cup smooth peanut butter (or almond butter)
½ cup pure maple syrup
¼ cup cacao powder, plus extra to sprinkle
3 tablespoons melted coconut oil
2 tablespoons coconut flour
2 teaspoons pure vanilla extract
¼ cup raisins
¼ cup crushed walnuts or pistachios
¼ teaspoon sea salt (optional)

Although they are primarily composed of sweet kūmara, you would never guess there was a vegetable hidden in these indulgently wholesome bites, which have the fudgiest, melt-in-your-mouth texture – similar to a brownie. In fact, I even played a little game with my family to see who could guess the main ingredient, and of course no one even came close! So easy to whip up, these fudgy bites are destined to become your new guilt-free, chocolatey snack.

Line a 20 cm x 28 cm (8 in x 11¼ in) baking dish with baking paper.

Bring a saucepan half-filled with water to a boil. Place the kūmara in a colander over the water, cover, and steam for about 15 minutes, or until tender.

Place the kūmara in a large bowl and mash until completely smooth. Add all the remaining ingredients and mix to combine.

Transfer the mixture to the prepared dish and spread out evenly. Using the back of a spoon, press firmly over the mixture to pack it down. Place in the freezer to set for about 1 hour.

To serve, remove from the freezer, sprinkle with extra cacao, if desired, and slice into 24 pieces.

Store in a sealed container in the fridge for 3–5 days, or in the freezer for up to 3 months.

MAKES 15 BLONDIES

WHOLESOME RASPBERRY BLONDIES

400 g (14 oz) can cannellini beans, drained and rinsed (or 1½ cups cooked beans)
¾ cup almond meal (ground almonds)
½ cup smooth peanut butter (or cashew or almond butter)
⅓ cup pure maple syrup
4 teaspoons pure vanilla extract
½ teaspoon baking powder
½ cup frozen raspberries, crushed

Wonderfully moist and sweet, and incredibly quick to come together, these yummy blondies very quickly became a firm favourite of Eli and Milo's. They particularly enjoy the creamy peanut butter flavour, but you can also use almond or cashew butter instead. The finishing scatter of crushed frozen raspberries provides a refreshingly sweet twist to these wholesome squares, which barely ever last a day in our home.

Preheat the oven to 180°C (350°F) fan-bake. Line a 20 cm (8 in) square baking dish with baking paper.

Place all the ingredients except the raspberries in a food processor. Blend for about 20–30 seconds, or until smooth. You may need to stop the food processor, scrape down the sides, then blend again.

Spoon the mixture into the prepared dish and spread out evenly. Sprinkle over the crushed raspberries and use the back of a spoon to press them slightly into the mixture. Bake for 30–35 minutes, or until golden then remove from the oven and let cool before slicing into 15 squares.

Store in a sealed container for 3–5 days.

MAKES 12 COOKIES

THE BEST LUNCH BOX CARROT CAKE COOKIES

1½ cups almond meal (ground almonds)
1 cup gluten-free rolled oats (or brown rice flakes)
1 cup coarsely grated carrot
½ cup shredded coconut
½ cup pure maple syrup
¼ cup sultanas
¼ cup chopped walnuts
1 teaspoon baking powder
1 teaspoon pure vanilla extract
1 teaspoon ground cinnamon
½ teaspoon mixed spice
½ teaspoon ground ginger
¼ teaspoon sea salt

These wonderful cookies mimic carrot cake quite perfectly, and I have to admit they're quite the moreish bite. Subtly spiced and perfectly moist, they make a fabulous and ridiculously easy lunch box cookie without the need for copious amounts of refined sugar. If you enjoy a lovely, moist carrot cake, you will definitely want to make this recipe. The quantities can easily be doubled to make a larger batch.

Preheat the oven to 180°C (350°F) fan-bake. Line a large baking tray with baking paper.

Place all the ingredients in a bowl and mix to combine.

Roll the mixture into 12 balls and arrange on the prepared tray. Press down on each cookie with the back of a fork. Bake for 25–30 minutes, then remove from the oven and let cool for 5–10 minutes before serving.

Store in a sealed container for 3–5 days.

RAW ZESTY WHOLEFOOD ENERGY BARS

MAKES 16 BARS

To my surprise, when I first made a batch of these nutritious energy bars, Eli's teenage mates found them quite the treat! With a sweet and lemony flavour, they're loaded with pure, raw nutrition that makes them a perfect grab-and-go fridge bar, lunch box addition or post-workout snack. You can dress them however you please or keep them as they are. The preparation is as easy as it gets; simply blend, set and slice!

Line a 20 cm x 28 cm (8 in x 11¼ in) baking dish with baking paper.

Place the dates in a bowl and cover with hot water. Soak for 15 minutes, or until they have softened. Drain and squeeze out all excess water.

Place all the ingredients, including the soaked dates, in a food processor. Blend for about 30 seconds, or until smooth. You may need to stop the food processor, scrape down the sides, then blend again.

Spoon the mixture into the prepared dish, spread out evenly then use the back of a spoon to press down firmly. Place in the freezer to set for about 1 hour.

To serve, remove from the freezer, top with shredded coconut and lemon zest, if desired, and slice into 16 bars.

Store in a sealed container in the fridge for up to 2 weeks, or in the freezer for up to 3 months.

1½ cups pitted dried dates
2 cups raw cashews
1 cup desiccated coconut
¼ cup hempseeds
¼ cup coconut flour
¼ cup lemon juice
3 tablespoons hulled tahini
1 tablespoon lemon zest
1 tablespoon pure vanilla extract
pinch sea salt

TO SERVE (OPTIONAL)
shredded coconut
extra lemon zest

MAKES 12–14 BALLS

RAW CHEWY GINGERBREAD COOKIE DOUGH BALLS

2 cups pitted medjool dates
1 cup almond meal (ground almonds)
½ cup almond butter
¼ cup coconut flour
1½ tablespoons cacao nibs (optional)
2 teaspoons pure vanilla extract
1½ teaspoons ground ginger
1 teaspoon ground cinnamon
½ cup desiccated coconut (for coating)

Craving something sweet but want the healthy benefits of raw, natural foods at the same time? Add these delish, doughy, gingery chews to your sweet-snack repertoire. Medjool dates, a super-healthy, naturally sweet fresh fruit are the main ingredient in this recipe – they are what give it its addictive chewy texture. High in many nutrients such as iron, potassium and B vitamins, dates also aid alkalisation with their favourable pH value. They're an incredibly wholesome addition to welcome into your pantry or lunch box, and here's a great prep-free tip: for a chewy, caramel-like sweet, medjool dates are irresistible when eaten straight from the freezer.

Place all the ingredients except the desiccated coconut in a food processor. Blend for about 30 seconds, or until smooth. You may need to stop the food processor, scrape down the sides, then blend again.

Using your hands, roll the mixture into 12–14 balls.

Sprinkle the coconut onto a large plate. Roll some or all of the balls through the coating.

Store in a sealed container in either the pantry or the fridge for up to 2 weeks, or in the freezer for up to 3 months.

MAKES ABOUT 20 PIECES

BLUEBERRY, LEMON AND CRANBERRY FROZEN YOGHURT BARK

BARK BASE
1 cup coconut yoghurt
¾ cup fresh or frozen blueberries
3 tablespoons pure maple syrup
3 tablespoons lemon juice
1 teaspoon pure vanilla extract

TOPPING
⅓ cup dried cranberries (or raisins)
¼ cup fresh or frozen blueberries
¼ cup shredded coconut
¼ cup pistachios

These simple, summery snaps are so easy and make a wonderful after-school (and after-dinner) snack. Simply blend, pour, dress and freeze! You can be as creative as you want with your topping ideas and easily mix up the flavours, too. The creamy bark can be frozen in a sealed container for up to 3 months, making it a great ready-to-go bite on those unexpectedly busy days.

Line a large baking dish with baking paper. (I used a 20 cm x 28 cm (8 in x 11¼ in) dish).

For the Bark base, place all the ingredients in a blender and blend for about 30 seconds, or until smooth. Pour into the prepared dish and spread out evenly.

To dress the bark, evenly scatter over the cranberries, blueberries, coconut and pistachios, and use the back of a spoon to lightly press these into the mixture if needed. Cover and freeze for 4–6 hours, or until set.

To serve, remove from the dish and break or cut into pieces of your desired size.

Store in a sealed container in the freezer for up to 3 months.

Tip: *This yoghurt bark will melt quickly so is best eaten straight from the freezer.*

PEAR AND POPPYSEED CASHEW CREAM

SERVES 2–3

This gorgeous, sweet fruity cream is delish drizzled over fresh, seasonal fruit. It makes a great brekkie, lunch box addition, after-school snack or dessert, and is easy to take out and about in a sealed jar. Make sure you blend the cream with very ripe pears to emphasise the beautiful fruity flavours.

Place all the ingredients except the poppyseeds in a blender and blend until smooth and creamy. Transfer to a small bowl and stir through the poppyseeds. Place in the freezer for about 30 minutes to firm up to a thick, spoonable consistency.

To serve, drizzle the Pear and Poppyseed Cashew Cream over bowlfuls of fresh fruit. Alternatively, place the fruit and cream into a large bowl and toss to combine. Garnish with mint, if using.

Store any leftover cream in a sealed container in the fridge for up to 5 days.

1 cup raw cashews, presoaked (see Recipe Notes page 42)
2 large very ripe pears, peeled and core removed
1 large banana, peeled and sliced
2 tablespoons pure maple syrup
1 teaspoon pure vanilla extract
1 tablespoon poppyseeds

TO SERVE
3–4 cups chopped fresh fruit (apples, pears, stone fruits, berries, pineapple, banana, etc.)
mint sprigs (optional)

DIPS AND DRESSINGS

DIPS AND DRESSINGS

This chapter is all about helping you to 'eat more plants' – as the popular mantra suggests! The valuable recipes on the following pages make this goal easy to achieve because the collection of healthy, game-changing dips and dressings will accentuate the plants on your plate and encourage you to eat more of them. In my experience, having a variety of delectable dressings on rotation plays a pivotal role in helping people (especially smaller children) embrace fresh vegetables regularly. They revolutionise the way raw plants can be enjoyed.

These handy recipes work all kinds of magic drizzled over fresh produce, salads, Buddha bowls and traybakes, or simply paired with a fresh platter of raw veggie sticks, wholefood crackers, wraps, tacos and more. As you know, a great dip or dressing can take any dish from ordinary to spectacular, but have you ever spent time looking at the ingredients listed on most store-bought condiments? The majority of them are loaded with unhealthy additives, refined sugars and thickeners that you most definitely want to avoid on a daily basis. The following quick and hassle-free recipes are a blend of natural ingredients working synergistically to create a selection of flavourful, crowd-pleasing dips and dressings that are sure to become much-loved kitchen staples.

PS. *If you want to create an oil-free dip or dressing, the majority of the oils in the following recipes can be replaced with water; please keep in mind the outcome and consistency will vary and may differ from the original recipe.*

MAKES 1½ CUPS

MANGO, GINGER AND LIME THAI DIP

1 cup diced mango (thawed, if using frozen mango)
½ cup coconut yoghurt
¼ cup hulled tahini
¼ cup lime juice
2 tablespoons pure maple syrup
1 tablespoon tamari
1 packed teaspoon finely grated fresh ginger
1 teaspoon onion powder
1 teaspoon apple cider vinegar
¼ teaspoon chilli flakes (optional)

When I first created this dreamy dip, I dived in with a generous handful of raw cabbage and avocado rolls and pretty much consumed the entire bowl! It features creamy mango, hints of ginger, zingy lime and a touch of chilli that, once blended together, morph into something really special. This dip partners well with Asian-inspired raw foods such as salads, rice paper rolls or fresh cabbage wraps. Feel free to use either thawed or fresh mango.

Place all the ingredients in a blender and blend for about 30 seconds, or until smooth and creamy.

Store in a sealed jar in the fridge for up to 5 days.

MAKES ABOUT 3 CUPS

SMOKY SPINACH CREAM CHEESE

750 g (1 lb 10 oz) fresh spinach leaves, roughly chopped (or baby spinach leaves)
1½ cups raw cashews, presoaked (see Recipe Notes page 42)
¾ cup water
½ cup nutritional yeast
½ cup lemon juice
4 cloves garlic
1½ teaspoons smoked paprika
½ teaspoon sea salt

This divine dip is an old favourite that resembles the popular spinach and feta filling, but with a twist. Absolutely chock-full of chunky green spinach immersed in a creamy mix of smoky, cheesy and lemony flavours, it's the perfect accompaniment to all things comforting. Hollow out the centre of a cob loaf and make it a built-in dip, dollop it into Buddha bowls or breakfast wraps, use it as a sandwich spread, or try it in the absolutely moreish Smoky Spinach Cream Cheese Smashed Potatoes on page 149 for a scrumptious dinner or appetiser.

Heat an extra-large saucepan over medium–high heat. Add the spinach along with a tiny splash of water and cook for about 5 minutes, stirring almost constantly, until the spinach is completely wilted. Remove and let cool. Squeeze out excess water and set aside

Place all the remaining ingredients in a blender and blend for about 30 seconds, or until smooth and creamy. Remove and pour into a bowl. Add the spinach and mix to combine well.

Store in a sealed jar in the fridge for up to 5 days.

INDIAN RAITA

MAKES 1½ CUPS

Similar to tzatziki, raita is a yoghurt-based condiment featuring cucumber. It is traditionally served with spicy dishes to cool the palate. This beautiful veganised take on this Indian dish is primarily composed of coconut yoghurt, cucumber, fresh herbs and aromatic spices. Together, they produce a refreshing dip that is especially good with spice-laden dishes. It's definitely worth making a batch to serve alongside my Tandoori Cauliflower, Jackfruit and Chickpea Bowls (page 162) for a flavourful feast.

Finely grate the cucumber and squeeze out as much liquid as you can. Place it in a small bowl along with all the other ingredients. Mix to combine well.

Store in a large jar in the fridge for up to 5 days.

½ large telegraph cucumber
1 cup coconut yoghurt
¼ cup finely sliced spring onion
3 tablespoons chopped fresh mint leaves
3 tablespoons chopped fresh coriander leaves
1 tablespoon lime juice
1 clove garlic, crushed or finely grated
½ teaspoon finely grated fresh ginger
½ teaspoon ground coriander
½ teaspoon ground cumin
½ teaspoon garam masala
¼ teaspoon sea salt

MAKES OVER 2½ CUPS

CHUNKY CASHEW AND SUNDRIED TOMATO PESTO

1 cup oil-free sun-dried tomatoes (see tip)
2 large red capsicums, halved and deseeded
1 large clove garlic
¼ cup lemon juice
¼ cup olive oil
3 tablespoons nutritional yeast
1½ tablespoons pure maple syrup
1 teaspoon onion powder
1½ cups raw cashews
sea salt (optional, see tip)

This tasty pesto is a firm favourite in our home. Eli and Milo particularly love it served with wholefood crackers. The cashews provide a crunchy textural component that adds a hearty element to this versatile dip. Try it alongside Buddha bowls and traybakes, or, for a delicious and easy wholesome lunch or light dinner, use it in my Cashew and Sun-dried Tomato Pesto Pasta with Fresh Basil and Avocado (page 126).

Place all the ingredients except cashews and salt in a food processor. Blend for about 40 seconds or until the mixture is mostly smooth. Add the cashews and pulse for a further 10 seconds, until the cashews are finely chopped. Adjust salt to taste.

Store in a sealed jar in the fridge for 5–7 days.

Tip: *I purchase my oil-free sun-dried tomatoes either online or from my local health food store. They can also be found in some supermarkets. They will likely contain more than enough salt already, but if not, you might like to add a little sea salt to this recipe.*

MAKES 1½ CUPS

SMOKY WHITE BEAN AND MISO HUMMUS

400 g (14 oz) can cannellini beans or chickpeas, drained and rinsed (or 1½ cups cooked beans or chickpeas)
2 cloves garlic
¼ cup lemon juice
3 tablespoons olive oil
2 tablespoons hulled tahini
2 tablespoons white miso paste
¾ teaspoon smoked paprika, plus extra to serve
¼ teaspoon sea salt

The great thing about this creamy hummus is you can either use white beans or chickpeas – whatever you have on hand. Thanks to the salty miso paste and smoky paprika, this bold, flavourful flourish will liven up a large platter of fresh veggie sticks or be equally fabulous lumped over traybakes and Buddha bowls.

Place all the ingredients in a food processor. Blend for about 30 seconds or until smooth, stopping to scrape down the sides of the food processor if necessary.

Store in a sealed jar in the fridge for up to 5 days.

MAKES 1½ CUPS

CUMIN AND THYME HUMMUS

400 g (14 oz) can chickpeas, drained and rinsed (or 1½ cups cooked chickpeas)
2 cloves garlic
¼ cup lemon juice
3 tablespoons olive oil, plus extra to serve
2 tablespoons hulled tahini
1 teaspoon ground cumin
¾ teaspoon dried thyme
½ teaspoon sea salt

I go through phases of being obsessed with eating generous dollops of this homemade hummus over a bed of raw and colourful produce and creamy avocado, with a sprinkle of chilli flakes. Lightly spiced with cumin and a hint of herby thyme, this has to be one of the most versatile and useful recipes for adding a touch of creamy flavour, depth and nutrition to any plate.

Place all the ingredients in a food processor reserving a few chickpeas for garnish. Blend for about 30 seconds or until smooth stopping to scrape down the sides of the food processor if necessary.

Store in a sealed jar in the fridge for up to 5 days.

MAKES 1½ CUPS

MOROCCAN CHERMOULA

1 cup fresh coriander
1 cup fresh parsley
½ cup fresh mint
¼ red onion
¼ cup olive oil
¼ cup lemon juice
2 large cloves garlic
1½ teaspoons ground cumin
1 teaspoon paprika
½ teaspoon ground coriander
¾ teaspoon sea salt
⅛ teaspoon cracked pepper

Moroccan chermoula is an effortlessly easy, herby condiment that comes in multiple variations and flavours. Texturally similar to pesto, this version is packed with spice-laden flavours that are contrasted by the large quantities of fresh herbs and zesty lemon. Enjoy this refreshing mingle served with warm and spicy food, roast veggies, traybakes and Buddha bowls, or check it out as part of this delicious salad: Moroccan Chermoula Millet with Roast Eggplant, Capers, Fennel and Pine Nuts (page 90).

Place all the ingredients in a food processor and blend for about 30 seconds, or until the mixture resembles a semi-smooth pesto. You will need to stop the food processor, scrape down the sides, then blend again.

Store in a sealed jar in the fridge for up to 5 days.

MAKES 1 CUP

CORIANDER CREAM

⅔ cup raw cashews, presoaked (see Recipe Notes page 42)
1 avocado, stoned and peeled
1 cup fresh coriander leaves
½ cup water
1 large clove garlic
3 tablespoons lime juice
1 teaspoon pure maple syrup
1 teaspoon garlic powder
½ teaspoon sea salt

If you enjoy a good guacamole, you'll love this recipe! It works amazingly well for dressing a salad, traybake or Buddha bowl. With time in the fridge, it will also firm up enough to be served as a wholesome dip. Oh, and I would definitely recommend it with my Chipotle Mexican Baked Jackfruit and Black Bean Salad with Coriander Cream (page 89).

Place all the ingredients in a blender and blend for about 30 seconds, or until smooth and creamy.

Store in a sealed jar in the fridge for up to 3 days.

AVOCADO MAYO

MAKES 1½ CUPS

Here's a super-quick and wholesome alternative to traditional mayonnaise. It gets its thick consistency and addictive creaminess from the nutritious avocado. Be sure to sample this delightful green dressing with my Epic Plant-Based Burger Patties (page 176).

Place all the ingredients in a blender and blend for about 30 seconds, or until smooth and creamy.

Store in a sealed jar in the fridge for up to 3 days.

1 avocado, stoned and peeled
¾ cup rice milk (or other plant milk)
2 tablespoons olive oil
2 tablespoons lemon juice
1 teaspoon wholegrain mustard
½ teaspoon garlic powder
½ teaspoon sea salt
¼ teaspoon ground white pepper

SWEET MUSTARD AND LEMON TAHINI DRESSING

MAKES 1½ CUPS

This is an ideal dressing to whisk together at the beginning of the week and keep in the fridge for an easy, ready-to-go salad dressing. I find its beautiful sweet and lemony flavours appeal to most, including my children. Try it drizzled over my Baked Yam, Caramelised Pecans and Rocket salad on page 98.

Place all the ingredients in a bowl and whisk until smooth and creamy, adjusting water to achieve desired consistency.

Store in a sealed jar in the fridge for up to 5 days.

Tip: *This dressing will naturally thicken with time in the fridge. Simply stir it to loosen prior to serving.*

½ cup hulled tahini
¼ cup lemon juice
¼ cup olive oil
3 tablespoons wholegrain mustard
3 tablespoons pure maple syrup
1–3 tablespoons water (depending on desired consistency)

MAKES 1½ CUPS

HEMP MISO AIOLI

½ cup sunflower seeds
⅓ cup hempseeds, plus extra to serve (optional)
¾ cup water
¼ cup white miso paste
6 tablespoons lemon juice
2 small cloves garlic
½ teaspoon ground ginger

I experimented with this tasty recipe recently and very quickly added it to my repertoire. Hempseeds have an earthy, nutty flavour and create an awesome creamy texture when blended. They also happen to contain a stellar list of beneficial nutrients. I especially love this dressing drizzled over the Cinnamon-spiced Kūmara, Quinoa and Rocket salad on page 106.

Place all the ingredients in a blender and blend for about 30 seconds, or until smooth and creamy.

Store in a sealed jar in the fridge for up to 5 days.

MAKES OVER 1 CUP

CREAMY DILL RANCH DRESSING

1 cup raw cashews, presoaked (see Recipe Notes page 42)
⅔ cup rice milk (or other plant milk)
1 packed tablespoon fresh dill, plus extra to serve (optional)
1 tablespoon wholegrain mustard
1½ tablespoons nutritional yeast
1 tablespoon lemon juice
2 teaspoons apple cider vinegar
1 tablespoon pure maple syrup
1 large clove garlic
½ teaspoon onion powder
⅛ teaspoon ground white pepper

One of those dressings that will seriously partner well with almost any dish, variations of this creamy ranch have been a long-time kitchen staple in our home. It's a great dressing to toss through any salad, including a quick homemade slaw. Definitely give it a whirl in these delicious recipes: Creamy Kale and Potato Wedges with Cranberries, Capers and Dill Ranch (page 110) or Waldorf Chickpea and Poppyseed Slaw (page 116).

Place all the ingredients in a blender and blend for about 30 seconds, or until smooth and creamy.

Store in a sealed jar in the fridge for up to 5 days.

MAKES 1 CUP

BEETROOT, MINT AND TAHINI YOGHURT

½ cup coconut yoghurt
¼ cup hulled tahini
¼ cup peeled and diced fresh beetroot
handful fresh mint, plus extra mint leaves to serve
2 cloves garlic
2 tablespoons lemon juice
2 tablespoons pure maple syrup
½ teaspoon sea salt

Not only is this dressing a beautiful way to add a touch of purple vibrancy to a dish, but it also adds a crisp and refreshing flavour. Quick and easy to throw together, this creamy yoghurt and tahini affair is a great way to include a hint of raw beetroot on your plate. It will complement any Middle Eastern cuisine, but also try it dolloped over Buddha bowls and traybakes.

Place all the ingredients in a blender and blend for about 30 seconds, or until smooth and creamy. Place in the fridge to set for about 30 minutes.

Store in a sealed jar in the fridge for up to 5 days.

Tip: This dressing will naturally thicken with time in the fridge. Simply stir it to loosen prior to serving.

MAKES ABOUT 1 CUP

EASY ALMOND COCONUT DRESSING

½ cup coconut yoghurt
¼ cup almond butter
2 tablespoons lemon juice
2 teaspoons pure maple syrup
1 teaspoon apple cider vinegar
2 small cloves garlic, crushed or finely grated
1 tablespoon water (optional for desired consistency)

This beautiful, creamy dressing was born on an evening when I was craving something new, and it quickly became a popular staple. It partners well with most recipes, and I love how fast and easy it comes together – you don't even need a blender.

Place all the ingredients in a bowl and whisk together until smooth and creamy.

Store in a sealed jar in the fridge for up to 5 days.

Tip: This dressing will naturally thicken with time in the fridge. Simply stir it to loosen prior to serving.

MAKES OVER 1 CUP

ROAST GARLIC DRESSING

¾ cup raw cashews, presoaked (see Recipe Notes page 42)
½ cup water
2 heads garlic (see tip)
2 tablespoons white miso paste
2 tablespoons lemon juice
1 tablespoon capers, drained
1 tablespoon pure maple syrup

When fused in a dressing, roast garlic has a completely different flavour profile to raw garlic. It imparts a beautiful, mild creaminess with a subtle garlic flavour, so don't be alarmed when you see the large quantities used in this recipe. This is an excellent choice to match with a traybake, Buddha bowl, hearty salad or pasta dish for an impactful depth of flavour.

Preheat the oven to 180°C (350°F) fan-bake. Line a small oven dish with baking paper.

To roast the garlic, peel any loose papery layers from each head, leaving the cloves intact. Slice horizontally across the top of the heads to expose the tops of each individual clove. Place, sliced-sides up, on the prepared dish and bake for about 45 minutes, or until heads are soft and brown. Once cooked, gently squeeze the cloves from their skins. They should slip out easily.

Place the roasted garlic in a blender along with all other ingredients, and blend for about 30 seconds, or until smooth and creamy.

Store in a sealed jar in the fridge for up to 5 days.

Tip: *For faster preparation, separate the garlic cloves, then remove the skin from each individual clove. Bake for about 10 minutes, or until soft. I prefer the longer cooking method as garlic skins are fiddly and tricker to remove when they are raw. I often roast the garlic heads ahead of time.*

SESAME DRESSING

MAKES ABOUT 1 CUP

If there was ever a way to eat the rainbow in large quantities of vibrant, raw veggies, it's drenched in a delicious Asian-inspired dressing like this one. I promise you'll finish the plate!

Place all the ingredients in a small bottle or glass jar with a lid and shake to combine.

Store in the sealed bottle or jar in the fridge for up to 5 days. Shake well prior to serving.

¼ cup sesame oil
3 tablespoons tamari
3 tablespoons pure maple syrup
3 tablespoons lime juice
3–4 tablespoons water
1 small clove garlic, crushed or finely grated
½ teaspoon finely grated fresh ginger
1 teaspoon sesame seeds

CREAMY SWEET CHILLI DRESSING

MAKES OVER 1½ CUPS

I have a weakness for sweet dressings that incorporate a touch of heat, which inspired me to create this creamy drizzle. It's a great dressing when you're in need of mixing up your flavours. It pairs especially well with roasted root veggies such as pumpkin, potato and kūmara, or gluten-free wholegrains for a nourishing salad.

Place all the ingredients in a blender and blend for about 30 seconds, or until smooth and creamy.

Store in a sealed jar in the fridge for up to 5 days.

Tip: *This dressing will naturally thicken with time in the fridge. Simply stir it to loosen prior to serving.*

¾ cup raw cashews, soaked (see Recipe Notes page 42)
⅓ cup rice milk (or other plant milk)
1 small red capsicum, halved and deseeded
2 tablespoons pure maple syrup
2 tablespoons lime zest
2 tablespoons lime juice
2 teaspoons finely grated fresh ginger
¼ teaspoon sea salt
¼–½ teaspoon chilli flakes

RAW TREATS

RAW TREATS

Craving an effortlessly easy, indulgent sweet ending to your meal without the aftermath of an upset tummy? This chapter has you covered with its delectable collection of unprocessed, raw treats, and their preparation couldn't be simpler. These decadent desserts are primarily composed of wholefood ingredients and are proudly refined sugar-free with zero artificial flavours and additives.

Although these recipes are designed to be occasional treats, I do realise that some of the ingredients are more expensive than the standard dessert recipes that call for regular flour and caster sugar. Most of the ingredients, however, are simple wholefood staples you may already have in your pantry. If not, bulk bins at health food stores can be a cost-effective way to purchase the exact quantity required for each recipe.

There is only one rule when it comes to my raw treats: they need to be stored in either the fridge or the freezer (take note of the specific recommendation I've made in each recipe) as they will melt fairly quickly when left at room temperature. Whether you choose to indulge in the rich, decadent chocolate treats, the silky-smooth caramel options or the creamy, fruit-based desserts, I'm confident there is a little something special awaiting you in the following dreamy pages.

LEMON AND MANGO CHEESECAKE

MAKES 1 CAKE

BASE
1 cup almonds
¾ tightly packed cup pitted medjool dates or presoaked dried dates (see Recipe Notes page 42)
¼ cup shredded coconut
1 tablespoon lemon zest
1 teaspoon pure vanilla extract
pinch sea salt

FILLING
2 cups raw cashews, presoaked (see Recipe Notes page 42)
400 ml (14 fl oz) can coconut cream
1 cup frozen mango pieces
⅓ cup pure maple syrup
⅓ cup lemon juice
3 tablespoons melted coconut oil
2 tablespoons lemon zest
1 tablespoon pure vanilla extract
few good pinches ground turmeric (for colour)

TO SERVE (OPTIONAL)
freeze-dried mango (see recipe intro)
extra shredded coconut
lemon zest

I'm mildly obsessed with the zesty, sweet tropical flavours featured in this delightful dessert. With no drop of dairy in sight, this cashew-based recipe has to be one of my all-time favourite plant-based desserts. And the best part? It's totally fuss-free and comes together so quickly and easily. It can be dangerously easy to devour this dreamy cake, but you won't endure that sick feeling you get from a refined-sugar overload. Although not essential, I highly recommend purchasing freeze-dried mango powder from your local health food store or online; I buy the Fresh As brand as it really does add that extra tropical touch.

Line the bottom of a 20–24 cm (8–9½ in) springform cake tin with baking paper. Lightly grease around the inside with coconut oil.

For the base, place all the ingredients in a large food processor and blend into a semi-fine texture. Tip the mixture into the prepared cake tin and press firmly to pack it down evenly.

For the filling, place all the ingredients in a blender and blend until smooth and creamy. Pour the mixture over the base and spread out evenly. Place in the freezer for 2–3 hours, or until the centre is firm.

To serve, remove from the cake tin and garnish with a sprinkle of freeze-dried mango powder, shredded coconut or lemon zest. If needed, place in the fridge to fully defrost before serving. It should be soft and creamy, not frozen. Slice and enjoy.

Store in a sealed container in the fridge for up to 5–7 days.

SENSATIONAL STRAWBERRY SORBET

SERVES 6–8

6 cups frozen strawberries
1 cup raw cashews, presoaked (see Recipe Notes page 42)
1 cup coconut cream
⅓ cup pure maple syrup
¼ cup coconut sugar
3 tablespoons melted coconut oil

TO SERVE (OPTIONAL)
fresh strawberries

Pretty pink and finger-licking good, this lovely sorbet-style soft-serve is definitely worth whizzing together. Honestly, all you need is some ripe, frozen fruit and a few other staple ingredients and you've got the most divine frozen deliciousness without overloading your body with dairy and copious amounts of refined sugars, artificial flavours and extra additives. There are endless flavours and combinations to explore, but I would definitely begin with this sweet strawberry bliss. If you don't plan on eating this sorbet immediately, just remember to let it soften out of the freezer prior to serving.

Place all the ingredients in a large food processor and blend for at least 2–3 minutes, or until smooth and creamy. You will need to stop the food processor, scrape down the sides, then blend again.

Tip the mixture into a sealed container or loaf tin, cover and freeze for 2–4 hours, or until firm.

To serve, remove from the freezer and, if needed, allow to soften before scooping with a hot ice-cream scoop (or spoon) into small serving bowls. Top with fresh strawberries, if desired.

Store any leftovers in a sealed container or loaf tin in the freezer. Prior to serving, remove from the freezer and allow it to soften for about 20 minutes.

Tip: *You can also serve this creamy strawberry blend as a sweet smoothie bowl. Simply spoon the mixture into bowls prior to freezing and serve with your desired toppings.*

MAKES 60 LOLLIES

RASPBERRY AND COCONUT ICE LOLLIES

2½ cups frozen raspberries
½ cup raw cashews
½ cup pure maple syrup
⅓ cup shredded coconut
¼ cup coconut cream (thick top layer)
1 tablespoon melted coconut oil

As the saying goes, 'once you pop you can't stop'! I had other plans for this epic recipe until magic occurred and these highly addictive super-sweet ice lollies were born. This simple recipe yields a large batch of lollies that can be stored in the freezer for up to 3 months, and these glistening frozen goodies are an easy treat for everyone, taking no more than 10 minutes to whip up. We love sucking on them as the delicious creamy textures dissolve.

Line a 20 x 28 cm (8 x 11¼ in) rectangular dish with baking paper.

Place all the ingredients in a large food processor and blend for about 45–60 seconds, or until smooth. You may need to stop the food processor, scrape down the sides, then blend again.

Tip the mixture into the prepared dish and spread out evenly. Freeze for about 2 hours, or until firm.

To serve, remove from the dish and slice into 60 lollies.

Store in a sealed container in the freezer.

Tip: *Just like an ice block, these lollies will melt fairly quickly outside of the freezer.*

CHUNKY SHORTBREAD TOFFEE BARS

MAKES 16 LARGE BARS, 24 SMALL BARS OR 48 BITES

Three indulgent layers. I begin with a prominent, extra-chunky shortbread base, follow up with a layer of sweet and chewy toffee and finish with a rich chocolate drizzle to create an addictive, decadent bar that is likely to become a popular family favourite. More often than not, the middle layer of a slice steals the limelight, but in this particular recipe, it shares the stage equally with the sweet and chunky biscuit base. It's one of my personal favourite treats in this chapter, I highly recommend these alluring fridge bars for all ages!

Line a 20 x 28 cm (8 x 11¼ in) rectangular dish with baking paper.

For the Biscuit base, place the ingredients in a large food processor and blend to a fine crumb-like texture. Tip the mixture into the prepared dish and press down firmly to pack evenly. If needed, quickly rinse the food processor bowl and blade.

For the Toffee layer, place the ingredients in the food processor and blend for at least 60–90 seconds to a smooth paste. You may need to stop the food processor, scrape down the sides, then blend again. Spoon the sticky toffee paste onto the base and spread evenly with a wet spatula or the back of a spoon. Place in the freezer for 1–2 hours to set.

For the Chocolate layer, heat a small saucepan over medium heat. Add all the ingredients and stir until the coconut oil is melted and the ingredients are combined. Remove from the heat. Remove the slice from the freezer and pour over the chocolate layer. Return to the freezer for 1 hour to set.

To serve, remove from the dish and slice into bars.

Store in a sealed container in either the fridge or freezer.

BISCUIT BASE

2 cups raw cashews
1 cup coconut flour
½ cup pure maple syrup
6 tablespoons melted coconut oil
2 teaspoons pure vanilla extract

TOFFEE LAYER

2 cups pitted medjool dates
⅓ cup almond butter
¼ cup pure maple syrup
3 tablespoons coconut oil
3 tablespoons water
2 teaspoons pure vanilla extract
pinch sea salt

CHOCOLATE LAYER

⅓ cup coconut oil
⅓ cup cacao powder
⅓ cup pure maple syrup

SALTED CARAMEL SLAB

MAKES 20 SQUARES

CHOCOLATEY BISCUIT BASE
1 cup raw cashews
⅔ cup almond meal (ground almonds)
3 tablespoons pure maple syrup
2 tablespoons cacao powder
2 tablespoons melted coconut oil
1 teaspoon pure vanilla extract

SALTED CARAMEL
1½ cups pitted medjool dates
1½ cups raw cashews, presoaked (see Recipe Notes page 42)
½ cup coconut cream (thick top layer)
½ cup pure maple syrup
⅓ cup hulled tahini
¼ cup melted coconut oil
3 tablespoons coconut sugar
1 tablespoon pure vanilla extract
1½ teaspoons sea salt (I use Himalayan)

CHOCOLATE TOPPING
¼ cup coconut oil
¼ cup cacao powder
3 tablespoons pure maple syrup

I bet you can't wait to sink your teeth into this silky-smooth slab. I have to admit, I put some extra time into perfecting this recipe because an indulgent caramel slice is always a popular pick. The key to the moreish, salted caramel layer is to patiently blend it for long enough (at least 4 minutes) to create the creamiest silky paste. Contrasted with a beautiful biscuit base and an easy chocolate topping, this irresistible slab can be enjoyed straight from the freezer as it won't completely freeze. For a softer, luscious texture, store it in a sealed container in the fridge.

Line a 20 cm (8 in) square dish with baking paper.

For the Chocolatey biscuit base, place all the ingredients in a large food processor and blend to a fine crumb-like texture. Tip the mixture into the prepared dish and press down firmly to pack evenly. If needed, quickly rinse the food processor bowl and blade.

For the Salted caramel, place all the ingredients in the food processor and blend for at least 4 minutes into a smooth paste. You will need to stop the food processor, scrape down the sides, then blend again. If it is easier, you can separate the ingredients into two batches. Spoon the thick caramel paste onto the base and spread evenly with a wet spatula or the back of a spoon. Place in the freezer for 2–3 hours to set.

For the Chocolate topping, heat a small saucepan over medium heat. Add all the ingredients and stir until the coconut oil is melted and the ingredients are combined. Remove from the heat. Remove the slice from the freezer and pour over the chocolate layer. Return to the freezer for 1 hour to set.

To serve, remove from the dish and slice into 20 squares.

Store in a sealed container in either the fridge or freezer.

Tip: *Remove the medjool dates from the fridge and allow them to soften at room temperature prior to blending.*

MAKES 20 SQUARES

FUDGY BROWNIE SLICE WITH PEANUT BUTTER VANILLA FROSTING

FUDGY BROWNIE
2 cups walnuts
1½ cups pittted medjool dates
½ cup cacao powder
½ cup coconut flour
⅓ cup pure maple syrup
¼ cup raisins
1 teaspoon ground cinnamon
½ teaspoon sea salt

PEANUT BUTTER VANILLA FROSTING
½ cup smooth peanut butter
¼ cup coconut cream (thick top layer)
¼ cup pure maple syrup
2 tablespoons coconut oil
2 teaspoons pure vanilla extract

TOPPINGS (OPTIONAL)
¼–½ cup chopped walnuts

To my dearest peanut butter lovers, this one's for you! I created this extremely easy recipe with everyone in mind because, seriously, who wouldn't enjoy a soft, chewy chocolate brownie with the fudgiest of textures and a smooth, peanut-buttery vanilla frosting to finish? If you're not a fan of peanut butter, don't worry, I've got you. Simply replace it with your preferred nut butter, such as almond or cashew butter, or omit the frosting altogether and enjoy this wholesome brownie in all of its solo glory (it's still amazing!). Whatever you decide, store this one in a sealed container in the fridge to maintain the perfect texture.

Line a 20 cm (8 in) square dish with baking paper.

For the Fudgy brownie, place the walnuts in a large food processor and blend for about 30 seconds, or until you have a fine crumb-like texture. Add all the remaining ingredients and blend until the mixture forms a dough-like ball.

Tip the mixture into the prepared dish and press down firmly to pack evenly.

For the frosting, heat a small saucepan over medium heat. Add the ingredients and stir until the coconut oil is melted and the ingredients are well combined. Pour over the brownie and spread out evenly. Scatter over the extra chopped walnuts, if using. Freeze for about 2 hours to set.

To serve, remove from the dish and slice into 20 squares.

Store in a sealed container in the fridge.

MAKES 1 CAKE

VELVETY CHOCOLATE MOUSSE CAKE

BASE
¾ cup almonds
10 large pitted medjool dates
2 tablespoons melted coconut oil
2 tablespoons cacao powder

CHOCOLATE MOUSSE FILLING
2 large ripe avocados, stoned and peeled
⅔ cup canned coconut milk
½ cup pure maple syrup
⅓ cup cacao powder
1 tablespoon melted coconut oil
1 teaspoon pure vanilla extract

TOPPINGS (OPTIONAL)
fresh strawberries
vegan chocolate, roughly chopped or grated

I'm sure you'll adore this rich, velvety cake just as much as we do. The natural creaminess of an avocado, a silent secret weapon in raw treats and dressings, is precisely the texture of this melt-in-your-mouth dessert. The delectable chocolate mousse can also be served with fresh berries for another wholesome dessert idea.
I like to dress this heavenly cake with lots of fresh strawberries, but for an impressive embellishment you could also add crushed or grated vegan chocolate.

Line the bottom of an 18–20 cm (7–8 in) springform cake tin with baking paper (or use a silicone pan). Lightly grease around the inside with coconut oil. Alternatively, line a loaf tin with baking paper.

For the base, place all the ingredients in a large food processor and blend to a semi-fine texture. Tip the mixture into the prepared tin and press down firmly to pack evenly.

For the Chocolate mousse filling, place all the ingredients in a blender and blend until smooth and creamy. Pour over the base and spread out evenly. Place in the freezer for about 3–4 hours, or until the cake is firm (not frozen).

To serve, remove from the tin and decorate with strawberries and chocolate, if desired. Slice and serve.

Store in a sealed container in the fridge.

MINT BOUNTY PISTACHIO SLICE

MAKES 16 SQUARES

What makes this slice so special is the combo of three mild but distinct layers that fit perfectly to create a heavenly mouthful of minty, coconutty and chocolatey goodness. I begin with a sweet hazelnut and cacao base, followed by a creamy peppermint and coconut filling, which is then slathered in a luscious chocolate ganache and finished with a light scattering of crunchy pistachios. If you love minty flavours, this really is a simple slice that works wonders for an after-dinner treat.

Line a 20 cm (8 in) square dish with baking paper.

For the base, place all the ingredients in a large food processor and blend to a semi-fine texture. Tip the mixture into the prepared dish and press down firmly to pack evenly. If needed, quickly rinse the food processor bowl and blade.

For the mint centre, place all the ingredients in the food processor and blend into a creamy mixture. Spoon the mixture onto the base and spread evenly. Place in the freezer for 1–2 hours to set.

For the chocolate topping, heat a small saucepan over medium heat. Add all the ingredients and stir until the coconut oil is melted and the ingredients are combined. Remove from the heat. Remove the slice from the freezer and pour over the chocolate layer. Finish with an even sprinkle of crushed pistachios. Return to the freezer for 1 hour to set.

To serve, remove from the dish and slice into 16 squares.

Store in a sealed container in the fridge.

Tip: *I use Dōterra pure essential peppermint oil in this recipe and I highly recommend it for the cleanest minty flavour. If using however, please follow the exact measurements I've given, as even 1 extra drop will create a big difference in flavour. To substitute, replace it with 1 teaspoon of pure mint extract.*

BASE
1 cup hazelnuts
10 large pitted medjool dates
2 tablespoons cacao powder
2 tablespoons coconut oil
2 teaspoons pure vanilla extract
pinch sea salt

PEPPERMINT BOUNTY FILLING
3 cups desiccated coconut
⅔ cup coconut cream (thick top layer)
½ cup pure maple syrup
3 tablespoons coconut oil
4 drops pure essential peppermint oil (see tip)
few pinches spirulina powder (optional, for colour)

CHOCOLATE GANACHE TOPPING
¼ cup coconut oil
¼ cup cacao powder
3 tablespoons coconut cream (thick top layer)
3 tablespoons pure maple syrup

TOPPINGS
¼ cup chopped pistachios

FULLY LOADED WHOLEFOOD ROCKY ROAD BARS

MAKES 16 BARS

½ cup coconut oil
½ cup pure maple syrup
⅓ cup plus 1 tablespoon cacao powder
1 tablespoon coconut flour
1 tablespoon pure vanilla extract
pinch sea salt
1 cup shredded coconut
¾ cup dried cranberries
½ cup raisins
½ cup hazelnuts
½ cup almonds
¼ cup hempseeds

This simple rocky road chocolate bar celebrates wholefoods and all the sweet and earthy goodness they provide. I love how versatile this recipe is; you can easily swap any of the chunky wholefoods with whatever you have available in your pantry. The numerous textural components add a little crunch and a touch of sweet chewiness, all suspended in a dark, decadent chocolate. These bars can either be stored in the fridge or the freezer for an on-the-go energising chocolate fix.

Line a 20 x 28 cm (8 x 11¼ in) rectangular dish with baking paper.

Heat a small saucepan over medium heat. Add the coconut oil, maple syrup, all of the cacao powder, the coconut flour, vanilla and salt and stir until the coconut oil is melted and the ingredients are combined. Remove from the heat. Add all the remaining ingredients and stir to combine into a thick mixture.

Tip the rocky road mixture into the prepared dish and spread out evenly. Freeze for 1–2 hours to set.

To serve, remove from the dish and slice into 16 bars.

Store in a sealed container in the fridge or freezer.

MAKES 24 PIECES

QUICK COCONUT ROUGH

½ cup coconut oil
½ cup pure maple syrup
⅓ cup cacao powder
1½ tablespoons coconut flour
2 teaspoons pure vanilla extract
pinch sea salt
2 cups shredded coconut, plus extra to serve

The sheer simplicity of this homemade chocolate will win you over every time. There is no need for a food processor – a small saucepan and about 5 spare minutes are all it takes to throw it together. I was once a little addicted to Dairy Milk chocolate (many moons ago now), and coconut rough was a particular favourite, so I thought I'd recreate a plant-based, wholefood version. The added coconut flour tones down the rich cacao to create a sweet confectionery without a drop of dairy, processed sugar or unwanted additives. Keep these squares in a sealed container in the freezer for a ready-to-go coconutty chocolate treat to satisfy those evening cravings.

Line a 20 x 28 cm (8 x 11¼ in) rectangular dish with baking paper.

Heat a small saucepan over medium heat. Add all the ingredients except the shredded coconut, then stir until the coconut oil is melted and the ingredients are combined. Remove from the heat. Add the shredded coconut and mix to combine.

Tip into the prepared dish and spread out evenly. Freeze for 1–2 hours to set.

To serve, remove from the dish sprinkle with extra coconut and slice into 24 pieces.

Store in a sealed container in the freezer.

SERVES 3

ORANGE MISO CARAMEL DRIZZLE WITH VANILLA WHIP

ORANGE MISO CARAMEL DRIZZLE
1 cup freshly squeezed orange juice
1 cup raw cashews (or macadamias), presoaked (see Kitchen Notes page 42)
½ cup coconut sugar
3 tablespoons hempseeds
2½ tablespoons white miso paste
1 tablespoon orange zest
1 teaspoon ground cinnamon

VANILLA WHIP
5 very ripe frozen bananas
¼–½ cup coconut water
1 tablespoon pure maple syrup
1 tablespoon hempseeds (optional)
1 teaspoon vanilla bean paste or pure vanilla extract

TOPPINGS (OPTIONAL)
coconut sugar
sliced fresh fruit

This delicious drizzle makes a delightful change from the standard (and often sickening) artificial caramel sauce. Featuring sweet-scented orange juice and a hint of earthy cinnamon, this fruity recipe creates a delectable dessert when drizzled over the creamy vanilla whip. White miso paste adds a subtle salty creaminess to this divine sweet sauce. You can easily find white miso in your local health food store.

For the Orange miso caramel drizzle, place all the ingredients in a blender and blend until smooth and creamy. Pour into a serving jug and set aside.

For the Vanilla whip, place all the ingredients in a high-powered blender or food processor and let sit for about 5 minutes to allow the bananas to slightly soften.

Start by blending on a low speed. Use a blending stick to assist with moving the bananas (if using a blender) then slowly increase to a high speed as the fruit begins to easily blend. You will probably need to stop the blender, mix and blend again, until you get a thick, creamy swirl.

To serve, spoon the Vanilla whip evenly into three bowls. Top each serving with a generous amount of Orange miso caramel drizzle and a light sprinkle of coconut sugar, if desired. Decorate each portion with a sliced orange and any other toppings such as banana coins or sliced strawberries.

WHOLESOME DOUBLE-CHOCOLATE CHIA PARFAITS

SERVES 6

This beautiful parfait features a rather rich raspberry base, which is perfectly contrasted by a creamy, coconutty chocolate topping. Together, they make for one indulgently blissful desert that imparts numerous health benefits – a win-win! Thanks to hempseeds and chia seeds, this superfood pudding boasts many essential nutrients including protein, iron, omega-3 fatty acids and fibre. We enjoy this chocolatey goodness at any hour of the day, including after school and in the evening. I pop it into the boys' lunch boxes, too.

For the Raspberry hemp pudding, place all the ingredients except the chia seeds in a blender and blend until smooth.

Transfer to a large bowl or a sealed container. Add the chia seeds and stir vigorously to combine well. Leave for 5 minutes, then stir again.

Repeat these steps for the Creamy coconut chocolate pudding.

Cover the two bowls then place both of them in the fridge for at least 2–3 hours or overnight, to set.

To serve, remove both bowls from the fridge and stir each of the puddings well to loosen. Spoon a layer of raspberry pudding into a small glass cup or jar, followed by a layer of coconut pudding. Top with a sprinkle of shredded coconut, crushed frozen raspberries, cacao nibs and/or sliced banana, if desired.

Store in a sealed container in the fridge for up to 5 days.

RASPBERRY HEMP CACAO PUDDING

1 large very ripe banana
1 cup frozen raspberries
1 cup plant milk (except coconut milk)
⅓ cup water
¼ cup pure maple syrup
¼ cup hempseeds
3 tablespoons cacao powder
⅓ cup plus 1 tablespoon chia seeds

CREAMY COCONUT CHOCOLATE PUDDING

2 large very ripe bananas
400 ml (14 fl oz) can coconut milk
½ cup water
¼ cup hempseeds
3 tablespoons pure maple syrup
3 tablespoons cacao powder
1½ teaspoons pure vanilla extract
⅓ cup plus 1 tablespoon chia seeds

TO SERVE

shredded coconut
frozen raspberries, crushed
cacao nibs
sliced banana

THANK YOU

Firstly, a mountain of gratitude and appreciation to my wonderful mum. This book would not have made it over the line without your love and support. Thank you so much for everything, Mum. You were my rock throughout and went above and beyond to help where possible. I would also like to extend a big thank you to my sister-in-law, Emma. You two were the absolute dream team in the kitchen — I couldn't have asked for more! You were both such a treat to work with and made the recipe shoot feel like a breeze.

To my beautiful boys, Eli, Milo and Jai. We created another book! Thank you for being so understanding and supportive as I worked hard on this project. You are forever my inspiration. And to Rich, thank you for always believing in me and encouraging me to be the best version of myself.

To my publisher, Jenny Hellen. Thank you for the opportunity to produce a second title, and for being so lovely and supportive throughout the entire process. It means the world that you believe in my books! And an enormous shout-out to Leonie Freeman and the rest of the team at Allen & Unwin, thank you for all the hard work you contribute behind the scenes. Also, a big thanks to Kate Barraclough and Katie Bosher for your invaluable input.

To my incredible photographer, Lottie Hedley. Thank you for all that you do; from capturing the beautiful images to prop styling and offering words of wisdom and advice along the way. It was truly an honour to work with you again.

To our lovely friends, Jasper and Anna Holdsworth. It was so special shooting at your beautiful batch in Mahia. Thanks so much for having us — what a magical spot! And to the team at Zephyr in Wainui; our community is so lucky to have a plant-based café that passionately shares delicious, wholesome food. Thank you for showering us in good vibes and epic smoothies during our photoshoot.

I would also like to express my gratitude to the following special people. Dean Buchanan, Nicole Breingan, Tracy Dibble, Shaun Tunny and Tim and Fleur Livingston. And a big shout out to Mahsa Willis from Mahsa the label, Lianne Whorwood from The Props Department and to everyone who generously offered fresh veggies from their gardens — thank you, thank you, thank you!

And lastly, to my wonderful readers and followers, and everyone who continues to support Raw and Free; thank you — I am endlessly grateful for you all!

INDEX

A
aioli, Hemp miso aioli 252
almond butter
   Almond miso glaze 140
   Almond miso-glazed eggplant boats with lime and basil rice salad 140
   Easy almond coconut dressing 254
   Gorgeous almond berry granola 210
   Pad Thai dressing 84
   Raw chewy gingerbread cookie dough balls 226
   Toffee layer 271
almonds
   Brown rice sesame sushi salad 124
   Cardamom-spiced yoghurt chickpea trail mix 204
   Creamy raw broccoli slaw 102
   Fully loaded wholefood rocky road bars 284
   Gorgeous almond berry granola 210
   Harissa yoghurt roast cauliflower chickpeas, rocket and toasted almonds 83
   Lemon and mango cheesecake 264
   Spiced roast cauliflower, green lentils and toasted almonds with smoky yoghurt 94
   Superseed snaps 214
   Velvety chocolate mousse cake 278
Antioxidant blueberry smoothie 58
apple
   Apple, lime and coriander chutney 143
   Waldorf chickpea and poppyseed slaw 116
   Winter wellness curried butternut and kūmara soup 158
   Vitamin boost green smoothie 54
apricot, Chunky lentil dahl with sweet apricot, roast cauliflower and fresh mint 134
avocado
   Avocado mayo 249
   Cashew and sun-dried tomato pesto pasta with fresh basil and avocado 126
   Chocolate mousse filling 278
   Coriander cream 246
   Creamy raw broccoli slaw 102
   Garlic broccoli, chickpeas, red chilli and rocket with turmeric tahini yoghurt 92
   Green goodness bowls 184
   Guacamole dressing 182
   San Clemente turmeric tofu and chickpea scramble bowls 166
   Simple, wholesome quinoa salad 113
   Supergreens chunky guacamole salad 114
   Teriyaki tofu poke bowls 160

B
Baked yam, caramelised pecans and rocket with sweet mustard and lemon tahini 98
baking
   Beautifully spiced banana bread 208
   Superseed snaps 214
   The best lunch box carrot cake cookies 220
   Wholesome raspberry blondies 218
Balsamic turmeric chickpeas 184
banana
   Antioxidant blueberry smoothie 58
   Banana blossom, leek and kūmara crustless pie with cheesy rosemary crumble 152
   Beautifully spiced banana bread 208
   Creamy coconut chocolate pudding 291
   Daily greens smoothie 54
   Mango lassi 56
   Mango, lime and raspberry smoothie 58
   Milo's PB and choc smoothie 61
   Mixed berry smoothie bowl with almond butter and granola 66
   My famous chocolate smoothie bowl 68
   Pear and poppyseed cashew cream 231
   Piña colada smoothie bowl 64
   Raspberry hemp cacao pudding 291
   Tropical strawberry smoothie 56
   Vanilla whip 288
   Vitamin boost green smoothie 54
   Wholesome Oreo smoothie 61
Banana blossom, leek and kūmara crustless pie with cheesy rosemary crumble 152
bars
   Chunky shortbread toffee bars 271
   Fully loaded wholefood rocky road bars 284
   Raw zesty wholefood energy bars 225
basil
   Cashew and sun-dried tomato pesto pasta with fresh basil and avocado 126
   Lime and basil rice salad 140
Beautiful raw marinated mushroom ceviche 120
Beautifully spiced banana bread 208
beetroot
   Beetroot, mint and tahini yoghurt 254
   Replenishing beetroot quinoa 123
berries *see also* specific berries
   Gorgeous almond berry granola 210
   Mixed berry smoothie bowl with almond butter and granola 66
bircher, Fully loaded pear and sultana birdseed bircher 213
biscuit
   Biscuit base 271
   Chocolatey biscuit base 272
black beans
   Chipotle Mexican baked jackfruit and black bean salad with coriander cream 89
   Jackfruit and black bean base 89
   Mexican kūmara wedges with hearty black bean guacamole salad 182
blondies, Wholesome raspberry blondies 218
blueberries
   Antioxidant blueberry smoothie 58
   Blueberry, lemon and cranberry frozen yoghurt bark 228
bok choy, Wholesome Chinese-style roast cashew red rice 174
Bombay jackfruit and crispy potato mingle with apple, lime and coriander chutney 143
bowls
   Mixed berry smoothie bowl with almond butter and granola 66
   My famous chocolate smoothie bowl 68
   Piña colada smoothie bowl 64
   San Clemente turmeric tofu and chickpea scramble bowls 166
   Tandoori cauliflower, jackfruit and chickpea bowls with creamy Indian raita 162
   Teriyaki tofu poke bowls 160
breads
   Beautifully spiced banana bread 208
   Garlic fennel flatbread 158
broccoli
   Creamy alfredo spaghetti with caramelised onion, broccoli and cheesy kale 146
   Creamy raw broccoli slaw 102
   Garlic broccoli, chickpeas, red chilli and rocket with turmeric tahini yoghurt 92
   Lemony miso millet, broccoli and edamame salad 78
   Post-surf jackfruit and kūmara red Thai curry 136
Brown rice sesame sushi salad 124
brownie, Fudgy brownie slice with peanut butter vanilla frosting 276
burgers, Epic plant-based burger patties with quick avocado mayo 176

SIMPLE WHOLEFOODS

C

cabbage
  Waldorf chickpea and poppyseed slaw 116
  Wholesome Chinese-style roast cashew red rice 174
cacao
  Chocolate ganache topping 283
  Chocolate layer 271
  Chocolate mousse filling 278
  Chocolate topping 272
  Chocolatey biscuit base 272
  Creamy coconut chocolate pudding 291
  Fudgy brownie slice 276
  Fully loaded pear and sultana birdseed bircher 213
  Fully loaded wholefood rocky road bars 284
  Milo's PB and choc smoothie 61
  Mint bounty pistachio slice 283
  My famous chocolate smoothie bowl 68
  Peanut butter kūmara fudge bites 216
  Quick coconut rough 286
  Raspberry hemp cacao pudding 291
  Raw chewy gingerbread cookie dough balls 226
  Velvety chocolate mousse cake 278
  Wholesome Oreo smoothie 61
cakes
  Lemon and mango cheesecake 264
  Velvety chocolate mousse cake 278
cannellini beans
  Smoky white bean and miso hummus 244
  Wholesome raspberry blondies 218
capers
  Creamy kale and potato wedges with cranberries, capers and dill ranch 110
  Delish lentil and caper traybake with mint and chilli yoghurt 157
  Moroccan chermoula millet with roast eggplant, capers, fennel and pine nuts 90
  Roast garlic dressing 256
capsicum
  Brown rice sesame sushi salad 124
  Chunky cashew and sun-dried tomato pesto 242
  Creamy harissa peanut satay noodles 172
  Creamy sweet chilli dressing 259
  Delish lentil and caper traybake with mint and chilli yoghurt 157
  Lime and basil rice salad 140
  Mediterranean ratatouille mingle 170
  Mediterranean smashed chickpea sandwich filler 194
  Mexican kūmara wedges with hearty black bean guacamole salad 182
  Pad Thai vermicelli noodle salad 84
  Pineapple salsa 181
  Post-surf jackfruit and kūmara red Thai curry 136
  Teriyaki tofu poke bowls 160
  Thai red curry sauce 136
  Wholesome Chinese-style roast cashew red rice 174
caramel
  Orange miso caramel drizzle 288
  Salted caramel 272
  Salted caramel slab 272
Caramelised onions 101
Caramelised pecans 98
cardamom
  Cardamom lime yoghurt 105
  Cardamom-spiced yoghurt chickpea trail mix 204
carrot
  Brown rice sesame sushi salad 124
  Cheesy carrot and chive raw oatmeal bites 199
  Creamy harissa peanut satay noodles 172
  Indian rice, carrot and roast cashew with cardamom lime yoghurt 105
  Pad Thai vermicelli noodle salad 84
  Quinoa and lentil balls 144
  Shepherd's pie filling 154
  The best lunch box carrot cake cookies 220
  Wholesome Chinese-style roast cashew red rice 174
cashews
  Biscuit base 271
  Cashew and sun-dried tomato pesto pasta with fresh basil and avocado 126
  Cheesy carrot and chive raw oatmeal bites 199
  Cheesy rosemary crumble 152
  Chocolatey biscuit base 272
  Chunky cashew and sun-dried tomato pesto 242
  Coriander cream 246
  Creamy alfredo sauce 146
  Creamy dill ranch dressing 252
  Creamy sweet chilli dressing 259
  Herby miso dressing 184
  Indian rice, carrot and roast cashew with cardamom lime yoghurt 105
  Lemon and mango cheesecake 264
  Orange miso caramel drizzle 288
  Pear and poppyseed cashew cream 231
  Raspberry and coconut ice lollies 268
  Raw zesty wholefood energy bars 225
  Roast garlic dressing 256
  Salted caramel 272
  Sensational strawberry sorbet 266
  Smoky spinach cream cheese 238
  Sumac pumpkin, caramelised onions and greens with roast garlic dressing 101
  Wholesome Chinese-style roast cashew red rice 174
cauliflower
  Chunky lentil dahl with sweet apricot, roast cauliflower and fresh mint 134
  Delish lentil and caper traybake with mint and chilli yoghurt 157
  Harissa yoghurt roast cauliflower chickpeas, rocket and toasted almonds 83
  Spiced cauliflower 94
  Spiced roast cauliflower, green lentils and toasted almonds with smoky yoghurt 94
  Tandoori cauliflower, jackfruit and chickpea bowls with creamy Indian raita 162
  Walnut and cauliflower 'chorizo' tacos with pineapple salsa 181
celery
  Creamy alfredo sauce 146
  Creamy kale and potato wedges with cranberries, capers and dill ranch 110
  Shepherd's pie filling 154
  Waldorf chickpea and poppyseed slaw 116
ceviche, Beautiful raw marinated mushroom ceviche 120
cheese
  Cheesy carrot and chive raw oatmeal bites 199
  Cheesy kale 146
  Cheesy rosemary crumble 152
  Eli's cheesy kale chips 203
  Smoky spinach cream cheese 238
  Smoky spinach cream cheese smashed potatoes 149
cheesecake, Lemon and mango cheesecake 264
chia
  Creamy coconut chocolate pudding 291
  Raspberry hemp cacao pudding 291
  Wholesome double-chocolate chia parfaits 291
chickpeas
  Balsamic turmeric chickpeas 184
  Cardamom-spiced yoghurt chickpea trail mix 204
  Cumin and thyme hummus 244
  Epic plant-based burger patties with quick avocado mayo 176
  Garlic broccoli, chickpeas, red chilli and rocket with turmeric tahini yoghurt 92
  Harissa yoghurt roast cauliflower chickpeas, rocket and toasted almonds 83
  Mediterranean smashed chickpea sandwich filler 194

Moroccan kūmara nuggets 169
Tandoori cauliflower, jackfruit and chickpea bowls with creamy Indian raita 162
Turmeric tofu and chickpea scramble 166
Waldorf chickpea and poppyseed slaw 116
chilli
   Apple, lime and coriander chutney 143
   Creamy sweet chilli dressing 259
   Garlic broccoli, chickpeas, red chilli and rocket with turmeric tahini yoghurt 92
   Mint and chilli yoghurt 157
Chipotle Mexican baked jackfruit and black bean salad with coriander cream 89
chives, Cheesy carrot and chive raw oatmeal bites 199
chocolate
   Chocolate ganache topping 283
   Chocolate layer 271
   Chocolate mousse filling 278
   Chocolate topping 272
   Chocolatey biscuit base 272
   Creamy coconut chocolate pudding 291
   Milo's PB and choc smoothie 61
   My famous chocolate smoothie bowl 68
   Velvety chocolate mousse cake 278
   Wholesome double-chocolate chia parfaits 291
'Chorizo' filling 181
Chunky cashew and sun-dried tomato pesto 242
Chunky lentil dahl with sweet apricot, roast cauliflower and fresh mint 134
Chunky shortbread toffee bars 271
Cinnamon-spiced kūmara, quinoa and rocket with hemp miso aioli 106
coconut
   Blueberry, lemon and cranberry frozen yoghurt bark 228
   Chocolate ganache topping 283
   Chocolate mousse filling 278
   Chunky lentil dahl with sweet apricot, roast cauliflower and fresh mint 134
   Coconut bakon 102
   Creamy coconut chocolate pudding 291
   Easy almond coconut dressing 254
   Fully loaded wholefood rocky road bars 284
   Gorgeous almond berry granola 210
   Lemon and mango cheesecake 264
   Mixed berry smoothie bowl with almond butter and granola 66
   My famous chocolate smoothie bowl 68
   Peanut butter vanilla frosting 276
   Peppermint bounty filling 283
   Piña colada smoothie bowl 64
   Quick coconut rough 286
   Raspberry and coconut ice lollies 268

Raw chewy gingerbread cookie dough balls 226
Raw zesty wholefood energy bars 225
Salted caramel 272
Satay sauce 172
Sensational strawberry sorbet 266
Superseed snaps 214
Thai red curry sauce 136
The best lunch box carrot cake cookies 220
Winter wellness curried butternut and kūmara soup 158
condiments
   Avocado mayo 249
   Hemp miso aioli 252
   Indian raita 241
   Moroccan chermoula 246
cookies
   Raw chewy gingerbread cookie dough balls 226
   The best lunch box carrot cake cookies 220
coriander
   Apple, lime and coriander chutney 143
   Coriander cream 246
corn
   Mexican kūmara wedges with hearty black bean guacamole salad 182
   Tasty corn and spinach fritters 196
crackers, Glazed black rice and sesame crackers 200
cranberries
   Blueberry, lemon and cranberry frozen yoghurt bark 228
   Creamy kale and potato wedges with cranberries, capers and dill ranch 110
   Creamy raw broccoli slaw 102
   Fully loaded wholefood rocky road bars 284
   Gorgeous almond berry granola 210
Creamy alfredo sauce 146
Creamy alfredo spaghetti with caramelised onion, broccoli and cheesy kale 146
Creamy coconut chocolate pudding 291
Creamy dill ranch dressing 252
Creamy harissa peanut satay noodles 172
Creamy kale and potato wedges with cranberries, capers and dill ranch 110
Creamy sweet chilli dressing 259
crumble, Cheesy rosemary crumble 152
cucumber
   Brown rice sesame sushi salad 124
   Green goodness bowls 184
   Hempseed tabouli 169
   Indian raita 241
   Simple, wholesome quinoa salad 113
   Supergreens chunky guacamole salad 114

Teriyaki tofu poke bowls 160
Cumin and thyme hummus 244
currants, Moroccan chermoula millet with roast eggplant, capers, fennel and pine nuts 90
curry
   Post-surf jackfruit and kūmara red Thai curry 136
   Thai red curry sauce 136
   Winter wellness curried butternut and kūmara soup 158

D

dahl, Chunky lentil dahl with sweet apricot, roast cauliflower and fresh mint 134
Daily greens smoothie 54
dates
   Fudgy brownie slice 276
   Lemon and mango cheesecake 264
   Mediterranean ratatouille mingle 170
   Mint bounty pistachio slice 283
   Raw zesty wholefood energy bars 225
   Salted caramel 272
   Toffee layer 271
   Velvety chocolate mousse cake 278
Delish lentil and caper traybake with mint and chilli yoghurt 157
dill, Creamy dill ranch dressing 252
dips
   Chunky cashew and sun-dried tomato pesto 242
   Coriander cream 246
   Cumin and thyme hummus 244
   Indian raita 241
   Mango, ginger and lime Thai dip 236
   Smoky spinach cream cheese 238
   Smoky white bean and miso hummus 244
dressings
   Beetroot, mint and tahini yoghurt 254
   Cardamom lime yoghurt 105
   Coriander cream 246
   Creamy dill ranch dressing 252
   Creamy sweet chilli dressing 259
   Easy almond coconut dressing 254
   Guacamole dressing 182
   Harissa yoghurt dressing 83
   Herby miso dressing 184
   Mint and chilli yoghurt 157
   Miso dressing 78
   Pad Thai dressing 84
   Roast garlic dressing 256
   Sesame dressing 259
   Smoky yoghurt dressing 94
   Sunflower cream dressing 102
   Sweet mustard and lemon tahini dressing 249
   Turmeric tahini yoghurt 92

E

Easy almond coconut dressing 254
eggplant
    Almond miso-glazed eggplant boats with lime and basil rice salad 140
    Mediterranean ratatouille mingle 170
    Moroccan chermoula millet with roast eggplant, capers, fennel and pine nuts 90
Eli's cheesy kale chips 203
Epic plant-based burger patties with quick avocado mayo 176

F

fennel
    Garlic fennel flatbread 158
    Moroccan chermoula millet with roast eggplant, capers, fennel and pine nuts 90
fillings
    Chocolate mousse filling 278
    'Chorizo' filling 181
    Mediterranean smashed chickpea sandwich filler 194
    Peppermint bounty filling 283
    Shepherd's pie filling 154
flatbread, Garlic fennel flatbread 158
fritters, Tasty corn and spinach fritters 196
frosting, Peanut butter vanilla frosting 276
fudge
    Fudgy brownie 276
    Fudgy brownie slice with peanut butter vanilla frosting 276
    Peanut butter kūmara fudge bites 216
Fully loaded pear and sultana birdseed bircher 213
Fully loaded wholefood rocky road bars 284

G

garlic
    Garlic broccoli, chickpeas, red chilli and rocket with turmeric tahini yoghurt 92
    Garlic fennel flatbread 158
    Roast garlic dressing 256
ginger, Mango, ginger and lime Thai dip 236
gingerbread, Raw chewy gingerbread cookie dough balls 226
glazes
    Almond miso glaze 140
    Glazed black rice and sesame crackers 200
    Tamari miso glaze 200
Gorgeous almond berry granola 210
granola, Gorgeous almond berry granola 210
greens
    Daily greens smoothie 54
    Green goodness bowls with balsamic turmeric chickpeas and herby miso dressing 184
    Sumac pumpkin, caramelised onions and greens with roast garlic dressing 101
    Supergreens chunky guacamole salad 114
    Vitamin boost green smoothie 54
Guacamole dressing 182

H

harissa
    Creamy harissa peanut satay noodles 172
    Harissa yoghurt dressing 83
    Harissa yoghurt roast cauliflower chickpeas, rocket and toasted almonds 83
hemp
    Hemp miso aioli 252
    Hempseed tabouli 169
    Raspberry hemp cacao pudding 291
herbs
    Herby miso dressing 184
    Moreish maple mustard crispy potato, mesclun and fresh herb salad 80
    Moroccan chermoula 246
hummus
    Cumin and thyme hummus 244
    Smoky white bean and miso hummus 244

I

ice lollies, Raspberry and coconut ice lollies 268
Indian raita 241
Indian rice, carrot and roast cashew with cardamom lime yoghurt 105

J

jackfruit
    Bombay jackfruit and crispy potato mingle with apple, lime and coriander chutney 143
    Chipotle Mexican baked jackfruit and black bean salad with coriander cream 89
    Jackfruit and black bean base 89
    Post-surf jackfruit and kūmara red Thai curry 136
    Tandoori cauliflower, jackfruit and chickpea bowls with creamy Indian raita 162

K

kale
    Cheesy kale 146
    Creamy alfredo spaghetti with caramelised onion, broccoli and cheesy kale 146
    Creamy kale and potato wedges with cranberries, capers and dill ranch 110
    Eli's cheesy kale chips 203
    Lentil base 94
    Spiced roast cauliflower, green lentils and toasted almonds with smoky yoghurt 94
    Sumac pumpkin, caramelised onions and greens with roast garlic dressing 101
    Supergreens chunky guacamole salad 114
kidney beans, Epic plant-based burger patties with quick avocado mayo 176
kūmara
    Banana blossom, leek and kūmara crustless pie with cheesy rosemary crumble 152
    Cinnamon-spiced kūmara, quinoa and rocket with hemp miso aioli 106
    Delish lentil and caper traybake with mint and chilli yoghurt 157
    Mexican kūmara wedges with hearty black bean guacamole salad 182
    Moroccan kūmara nuggets 169
    Peanut butter kūmara fudge bites 216
    Post-surf jackfruit and kūmara red Thai curry 136
    Winter wellness curried butternut and kūmara soup 158

L

leek, Banana blossom, leek and kūmara crustless pie with cheesy rosemary crumble 152
lemon
    Blueberry, lemon and cranberry frozen yoghurt bark 228
    Lemon and mango cheesecake 264
    Lemony miso millet, broccoli and edamame salad 78
    Miso dressing 78
    Raw zesty wholefood energy bars 225
    Sweet mustard and lemon tahini dressing 249
lentils
    Chunky lentil dahl with sweet apricot, roast cauliflower and fresh mint 134
    Delish lentil and caper traybake with mint and chilli yoghurt 157
    Lentil base 94
    Quinoa and lentil balls 144
    Shepherd's pie filling 154
    Spiced roast cauliflower, green lentils and toasted almonds with smoky yoghurt 94
lime
    Apple, lime and coriander chutney 143
    Cardamom lime yoghurt 105

Creamy sweet chilli dressing 259
Guacamole dressing 182
Lime and basil rice salad 140
Mango, ginger and lime Thai dip 236
Mango, lime and raspberry smoothie 58
Mint and chilli yoghurt 157
Satay sauce 172

M

mango
Daily greens smoothie 54
Lemon and mango cheesecake 264
Mango, ginger and lime Thai dip 236
Mango lassi 56
Mango, lime and raspberry smoothie 58
Tropical strawberry smoothie 56

maple syrup
Maple mustard potatoes 80
Moreish maple mustard crispy potato, mesclun and fresh herb salad 80

Marinade 120
Marinara sauce 144
mayo, Avocado mayo 249
Mediterranean ratatouille mingle with thyme and cumin hummus 170
Mediterranean smashed chickpea sandwich filler 194
Mexican kūmara wedges with hearty black bean guacamole salad 182

millet
Lemony miso millet, broccoli and edamame salad 78
Moroccan chermoula millet with roast eggplant, capers, fennel and pine nuts 90

Milo's PB and choc smoothie 61

mint
Beetroot, mint and tahini yoghurt 254
Chunky lentil dahl with sweet apricot, roast cauliflower and fresh mint 134
Mint and chilli yoghurt 157
Mint bounty pistachio slice 283

miso
Almond miso glaze 140
Cheesy rosemary crumble 152
Hemp miso aioli 252
Herby miso dressing 184
Lemony miso millet, broccoli and edamame salad 78
Miso dressing 78
Orange miso caramel drizzle 288
Roast garlic dressing 256
Smoky white bean and miso hummus 244
Sunflower cream 152
Tamari miso glaze 200
Wholesome Chinese-style roast cashew red rice 174

Mixed berry smoothie bowl with almond butter and granola 66
Moreish maple mustard crispy potato, mesclun and fresh herb salad 80
Moroccan chermoula 246
Moroccan chermoula millet with roast eggplant, capers, fennel and pine nuts 90
Moroccan kūmara nuggets with wholesome hempseed tabouli 169

mousse
Chocolate mousse filling 278
Velvety chocolate mousse cake 278

mushrooms
Beautiful raw marinated mushroom ceviche 120
Shepherd's pie filling 154

mustard
Maple mustard potatoes 80
Marinade 120
Moreish maple mustard crispy potato, mesclun and fresh herb salad 80
Sweet mustard and lemon tahini dressing 249

My famous chocolate smoothie bowl 68

N

noodles
Creamy harissa peanut satay noodles 172
Pad Thai vermicelli noodle salad 84

nuggets, Moroccan kūmara nuggets 169

O

oats
Cheesy carrot and chive raw oatmeal bites 199
The best lunch box carrot cake cookies 220

olives
Cashew and sun-dried tomato pesto pasta with fresh basil and avocado 126
Chipotle Mexican baked jackfruit and black bean salad with coriander cream 89
Mediterranean ratatouille mingle 170
Mediterranean smashed chickpea sandwich filler 194
Mexican kūmara wedges with hearty black bean guacamole salad 182
Moroccan kūmara nuggets 169

onions
Caramelised onions 101
Creamy alfredo spaghetti with caramelised onion, broccoli and cheesy kale 146
Sumac pumpkin, caramelised onions and greens with roast garlic dressing 101

orange
Orange miso caramel drizzle with vanilla whip 288
Vitamin boost green smoothie 54

P

Pad Thai dressing 84
Pad Thai vermicelli noodle salad 84
parfait, Wholesome double-chocolate chia parfaits 291

pasta
Cashew and sun-dried tomato pesto pasta with fresh basil and avocado 126
Creamy alfredo spaghetti with caramelised onion, broccoli and cheesy kale 146

peanut butter
Creamy harissa peanut satay noodles 172
Milo's PB and choc smoothie 61
Peanut butter kūmara fudge bites 216
Peanut butter vanilla frosting 276
Satay sauce 172
Thai red curry sauce 136
Wholesome raspberry blondies 218

peanuts, Pad Thai vermicelli noodle salad 84

pear
Fully loaded pear and sultana birdseed bircher 213
Pear and poppyseed cashew cream 231

peas, Wholesome Chinese-style roast cashew red rice 174
pecans, Baked yam, caramelised pecans and rocket with sweet mustard and lemon tahini 98
Peppermint bounty filling 283

pesto
Cashew and sun-dried tomato pesto pasta with fresh basil and avocado 126
Chunky cashew and sun-dried tomato pesto 242

pies
Banana blossom, leek and kūmara crustless pie with cheesy rosemary crumble 152
The ultimate hearty and flavourful vegan shepherd's pie 154

Piña colada smoothie bowl 64

pineapple
Daily greens smoothie 54
Piña colada smoothie bowl 64
Pineapple salsa 181
Tropical strawberry smoothie 56

pine nuts
Garlic broccoli, chickpeas, red chilli and rocket with turmeric tahini yoghurt 92
Moroccan chermoula millet with roast eggplant, capers, fennel and pine nuts 90

pistachios
    Blueberry, lemon and cranberry frozen yoghurt bark 228
    Cinnamon-spiced kūmara, quinoa and rocket with hemp miso aioli 106
    Mint bounty pistachio slice 283
    Moroccan kūmara nuggets 169
poppyseeds
    Pear and poppyseed cashew cream 231
    Waldorf chickpea and poppyseed slaw 116
Post-surf jackfruit and kūmara red Thai curry 136
potato
    Bombay jackfruit and crispy potato mingle with apple, lime and coriander chutney 143
    Creamy kale and potato wedges with cranberries, capers and dill ranch 110
    Delish lentil and caper traybake with mint and chilli yoghurt 157
    Maple mustard potatoes 80
    Mediterranean ratatouille mingle 170
    Moreish maple mustard crispy potato, mesclun and fresh herb salad 80
    Potato topping 154
    Smoky spinach cream cheese smashed potatoes 149
puddings
    Creamy coconut chocolate pudding 291
    Raspberry hemp cacao pudding 291
pumpkin
    Sumac pumpkin, caramelised onions and greens with roast garlic dressing 101
    Winter wellness curried butternut and kūmara soup 158

Q

Quick coconut rough 286
quinoa
    Cinnamon-spiced kūmara, quinoa and rocket with hemp miso aioli 106
    Quinoa and lentil balls 144
    Replenishing beetroot quinoa 123
    San Clemente turmeric tofu and chickpea scramble bowls 166
    Simple, wholesome quinoa salad 113

R

raspberry
    Mango, lime and raspberry smoothie 58
    Raspberry and coconut ice lollies 268
    Raspberry hemp cacao pudding 291
    Wholesome raspberry blondies 218
ratatouille, Mediterranean ratatouille mingle 170
Raw chewy gingerbread cookie dough balls 226

Raw zesty wholefood energy bars 225
Replenishing beetroot quinoa 123
rice
    Brown rice sesame sushi salad 124
    Fully loaded pear and sultana birdseed bircher 213
    Glazed black rice and sesame crackers 200
    Gorgeous almond berry granola 210
    Green goodness bowls with balsamic turmeric chickpeas and herby miso dressing 184
    Indian rice, carrot and roast cashew with cardamom lime yoghurt 105
    Lime and basil rice salad 140
    Teriyaki tofu poke bowls 160
    Wholesome Chinese-style roast cashew red rice 174
Roast garlic dressing 256
rocket
    Baked yam, caramelised pecans and rocket with sweet mustard and lemon tahini 98
    Cinnamon-spiced kūmara, quinoa and rocket with hemp miso aioli 106
    Garlic broccoli, chickpeas, red chilli and rocket with turmeric tahini yoghurt 92
    Harissa yoghurt roast cauliflower chickpeas, rocket and toasted almonds 83
    San Clemente turmeric tofu and chickpea scramble bowls 166
rosemary, Cheesy rosemary crumble 152

S

salsa, Pineapple salsa 181
Salted caramel 272
Salted caramel slab 272
San Clemente turmeric tofu and chickpea scramble bowls 166
Satay sauce 172
sauces
    Creamy alfredo sauce 146
    Marinara sauce 144
    Teriyaki sauce 160
    Thai red curry sauce 136
seeds
    Antioxidant blueberry smoothie 58
    Cardamom-spiced yoghurt chickpea trail mix 204
    Cheesy carrot and chive raw oatmeal bites 199
    Daily greens smoothie 54
    Fully loaded pear and sultana birdseed bircher 213
    Fully loaded wholefood rocky road bars 284

Hemp miso aioli 252
Mango lassi 56
Mango, lime and raspberry smoothie 58
My famous chocolate smoothie bowl 68
Orange miso caramel drizzle 288
Raw zesty wholefood energy bars 225
Sunflower cream 152
Sunflower cream dressing 102
Superseed snaps 214
Wholesome Oreo smoothie 61
Sensational strawberry sorbet 266
sesame
    Brown rice sesame sushi salad 124
    Cheesy rosemary crumble 152
    Glazed black rice and sesame crackers 200
    Sesame dressing 259
Shepherd's pie filling 154
shortbread, Chunky shortbread toffee bars 271
Simple, wholesome quinoa salad 113
slab, Salted caramel slab 272
slaws
    Creamy raw broccoli slaw 102
    Waldorf chickpea and poppyseed slaw 116
slice
    Fudgy brownie slice with peanut butter vanilla frosting 276
    Mint bounty pistachio slice 283
Smoky coconut bakon and creamy raw broccoli slaw 102
Smoky spinach cream cheese 238
Smoky spinach cream cheese smashed potatoes 149
Smoky white bean and miso hummus 244
Smoky yoghurt dressing 94
smoothies
    Antioxidant blueberry smoothie 58
    Daily greens smoothie 54
    Mango lassi 56
    Mango, lime and raspberry smoothie 58
    Milo's PB and choc smoothie 61
    Mixed berry smoothie bowl with almond butter and granola 66
    My famous chocolate smoothie bowl 68
    Piña colada smoothie bowl 64
    Tropical strawberry smoothie 56
    Vitamin boost green smoothie 54
    Wholesome Oreo smoothie 61
sorbet, Sensational strawberry sorbet 266
soup, Winter wellness curried butternut and kūmara soup 158
Spiced cauliflower 94
Spiced roast cauliflower, green lentils and toasted almonds with smoky yoghurt 94
spinach
    Banana blossom, leek and kūmara

crustless pie with cheesy rosemary crumble 152
Bombay jackfruit and crispy potato mingle with apple, lime and coriander chutney 143
Chipotle Mexican baked jackfruit and black bean salad with coriander cream 89
Chunky lentil dahl with sweet apricot, roast cauliflower and fresh mint 134
Creamy harissa peanut satay noodles 172
Daily greens smoothie 54
Herby miso dressing 184
Moroccan chermoula millet with roast eggplant, capers, fennel and pine nuts 90
Simple, wholesome quinoa salad 113
Smoky spinach cream cheese 238
Smoky spinach cream cheese smashed potatoes 149
Sumac pumpkin, caramelised onions and greens with roast garlic dressing 101
Supergreens chunky guacamole salad 114
Tasty corn and spinach fritters 196
Vitamin boost green smoothie 54
strawberries
	Sensational strawberry sorbet 266
	Tropical strawberry smoothie 56
sugar snap peas, Creamy harissa peanut satay noodles 172
Supergreens chunky guacamole salad 114
Superseed snaps 214
sushi, Brown rice sesame sushi salad 124
Sweet mustard and lemon tahini dressing 249

T

tabouli, Hempseed tabouli 169
tacos, Walnut and cauliflower 'chorizo' tacos with pineapple salsa 181
tahini
	Beetroot, mint and tahini yoghurt 254
	Cheesy carrot and chive raw oatmeal bites 199
	Cumin and thyme hummus 244
	Mango, ginger and lime Thai dip 236
	Mediterranean smashed chickpea sandwich filler 194
	Raw zesty wholefood energy bars 225
	Salted caramel 272
	Smoky white bean and miso hummus 244
	Sweet mustard and lemon tahini dressing 249
	Turmeric tahini yoghurt 92
Tamari miso glaze 200
Tandoori cauliflower, jackfruit and chickpea bowls with creamy Indian raita 162
Tasty corn and spinach fritters 196

Tasty quinoa and lentil balls with easy marinara sauce 144
Teriyaki sauce 160
Teriyaki tofu poke bowls 160
Thai red curry sauce 136
The best lunch box carrot cake cookies 220
The ultimate hearty and flavourful vegan shepherd's pie 154
thyme, Cumin and thyme hummus 244
toffee
	Chunky shortbread toffee bars 271
	Toffee layer 271
tofu
	Teriyaki tofu poke bowls 160
	Turmeric tofu and chickpea scramble 166
tomatoes
	Cashew and sun-dried tomato pesto pasta with fresh basil and avocado 126
	Chunky cashew and sun-dried tomato pesto 242
	Hempseed tabouli 169
	Marinara sauce 144
	Mexican kūmara wedges with hearty black bean guacamole salad 182
	San Clemente turmeric tofu and chickpea scramble bowls 166
	Simple, wholesome quinoa salad 113
	Supergreens chunky guacamole salad 114
toppings
	Chocolate ganache topping 283
	Chocolate topping 272
	Potato topping 154
trail mix, Cardamom-spiced yoghurt chickpea trail mix 204
traybake, Delish lentil and caper traybake with mint and chilli yoghurt 157
Tropical strawberry smoothie 56
turmeric
	Balsamic turmeric chickpeas 184
	Turmeric tahini yoghurt 92
	Turmeric tofu and chickpea scramble 166

V

vanilla
	Peanut butter vanilla frosting 276
	Vanilla whip 288
Velvety chocolate mousse cake 278
Vitamin boost green smoothie 54

W

Waldorf chickpea and poppyseed slaw 116
walnuts
	Beautifully spiced banana bread 208
	Fudgy brownie slice 276
	Peanut butter kūmara fudge bites 216
	The best lunch box carrot cake cookies 220

	Waldorf chickpea and poppyseed slaw 116
	Walnut and cauliflower 'chorizo' tacos with pineapple salsa 181
Wholesome Chinese-style roast cashew red rice 174
Wholesome double-chocolate chia parfaits 291
Wholesome Oreo smoothie 61
Wholesome raspberry blondies 218
Winter wellness curried butternut and kūmara soup with garlic fennel flatbread 158

Y

yams, Baked yam, caramelised pecans and rocket with sweet mustard and lemon tahini 98
yoghurt
	Beetroot, mint and tahini yoghurt 254
	Blueberry, lemon and cranberry frozen yoghurt bark 228
	Cardamom lime yoghurt 105
	Cardamom-spiced yoghurt chickpea trail mix 204
	Easy almond coconut dressing 254
	Harissa yoghurt dressing 83
	Indian raita 241
	Mango, ginger and lime Thai dip 236
	Mango lassi 56
	Mint and chilli yoghurt 157
	Smoky yoghurt dressing 94
	Tasty corn and spinach fritters 196
	Turmeric tahini yoghurt 92

Z

zucchini
	Mediterranean ratatouille mingle 170
	Shepherd's pie filling 154
	Sumac pumpkin, caramelised onions and greens with roast garlic dressing 101

First published in 2022

Text © Sophie Steevens, 2022
Photography © Lottie Hedley, 2022
(except pages 44/45, 62/63, 138/139 and 222/223 © Shaun Tunny)

All rights reserved. No part of this book may be reproduced or transmitted in any form or by any means, electronic or mechanical, including photocopying, recording or by any information storage and retrieval system, without prior permission in writing from the publisher.

Allen & Unwin
Level 2, 10 College Hill
Auckland 1011, New Zealand
Phone: (64 9) 377 3800
Email: info@allenandunwin.com
Web: allenandunwin.co.nz

83 Alexander Street
Crows Nest NSW 2065, Australia
Phone: (61 2) 8425 0100

A catalogue record for this book is available from the National Library of New Zealand

ISBN 978 1 98854 787 9

Design by Kate Barraclough
Set in 10/14 pt Brandon Text
Food styling: Sophie Steevens
Prop styling: Lottie Hedley and Sophie Steevens
Printed and bound in China by C&C Printing Co Ltd

10 9 8 7 6 5 4 3 2 1